HOLIDAY ORIGAMI

More Hanukkah Origami

by Ruth Owen

PowerKiDS press™

New York

Published in 2015 by
The Rosen Publishing Group, Inc.
29 East 21st Street, New York, NY 10010

Library of Congress Cataloging-in-Publication Data

Owen, Ruth.
More Hanukkah origami / by Ruth Owen.
p. cm. — (Holiday origami)
Includes index.
ISBN 978-1-4777-5715-4 (pbk.)
ISBN 978-1-4777-5716-1 (6-pack)
ISBN 978-1-4777-5714-7 (library binding)
1. Origami — Juvenile literature. 2. Hanukkah decorations — Juvenile literature.
I. Owen, Ruth, 1967-. II. Title.
TT870.O94 2015
736.982—d23

Produced for Rosen by Ruby Tuesday Books Ltd
Editor for Ruby Tuesday Books Ltd: Mark J. Sachner
US Editor: Sara Antill
Designer: Emma Randall

Photo Credits:
Cover, 1, 3, 5, 7, 8, 28 © Shutterstock.

Origami models © Ruby Tuesday Books Ltd.

Manufactured in the United States of America

CPSIA Compliance Information: Batch # CW15PK: For Further Information contact Rosen Publishing, New York, New York at 1-800-237-9932

Contents

Origami in Action

Hanukkah is a wonderful time for family and friends to celebrate with gifts, blessings, burning candles, and food. It's also a great time to get creative with **origami**.

Origami is the art of folding paper to make small **sculptures**, or models. This popular art form gets its name from the Japanese words "ori," which means "folding," and "kami," which means "paper." People have been making origami models in Japan for hundreds of years.

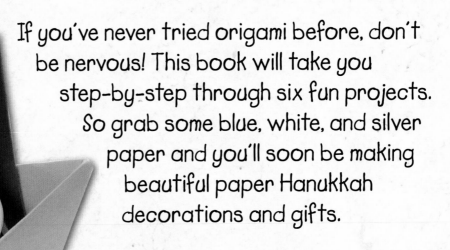

If you've never tried origami before, don't be nervous! This book will take you step-by-step through six fun projects. So grab some blue, white, and silver paper and you'll soon be making beautiful paper Hanukkah decorations and gifts.

Get Folding!

Before you get started on your Hanukkah origami models, here are some tips.

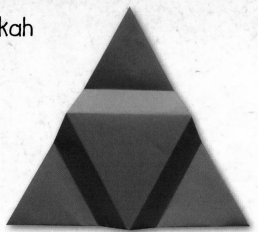

Tip 1

Read all the instructions carefully and look at the pictures. Make sure you understand what's required before you begin a fold. Don't rush; be patient. Work slowly and carefully.

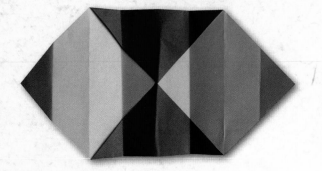

Tip 2

Folding a piece of paper sounds easy, but it can be tricky to get neat, accurate folds. The more you practice, the easier it becomes.

Tip 3

If an instruction says "crease," make the crease as flat as possible. The flatter the creases, the better the model. You can make a sharp crease by running a plastic ruler along the edge of the paper.

Tip 4

Sometimes, at first, your models may look a little crumpled. Don't give up! The more models you make, the better you will get at folding and creasing.

When it comes to origami, practice makes perfect!

In this book, you will find instructions for making stars and gift boxes. Just take a look at the complicated gift box and stars on this page. These models were made by experienced origami model makers. Keep practicing and you could become an origami master and soon be making difficult models like these!

When you turn the page, you'll find instructions for making paper Stars of David. You can turn your origami stars into a hanging decoration. All you need to do is use clothespins and a piece of string to create a decoration that's quick to make but has a cool vintage look!

Origami Star of David

The six-pointed Star of David has been used as a **symbol** on Jewish prayer books, religious objects, and buildings for more than 1,000 years. The star has also been an **emblem** of the Jewish people.

The Star of David is usually shown in blue and white. These colors are also associated with the Jewish people. Blue and white are the colors of the *tallit*, the prayer shawl worn over the shoulders at Jewish Sabbath, holiday, and morning services.

In this first project you will learn how to make origami six-pointed stars using blue and white paper.

A Star of David symbol on a Jewish synagogue, or temple

To make a Star of David, you will need:

One sheet of paper that's blue, white, or silver

(Origami paper is sometimes colored on both sides or white on one side.)

STEP 1:
Begin with a piece of paper that is rectangular.

STEP 2:
Place the paper colored-side down, fold in half, and crease.

STEP 3:
Unfold the crease you've just made. Now fold down the top left-hand corner so that the point touches the center crease and the bottom left-hand corner forms a sharp point. Crease well.

Top left-hand point should touch the center crease.

The bottom left-hand corner should form a point once the fold is made.

9

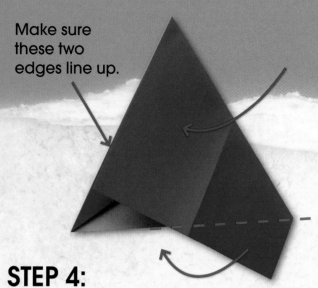

Make sure these two edges line up.

STEP 4:

Now fold down the top right-hand corner of the model so that it forms a triangle shape and the two edges of the paper line up on the left-hand side. Crease well.

Fold up the bottom right-hand point of the model along the dotted line, and tuck it inside the model.

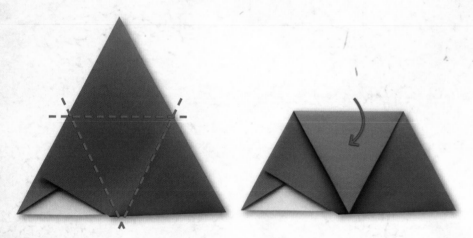

STEP 5:

Fold down the top point of the model so it meets the base of the model, crease hard, and unfold.

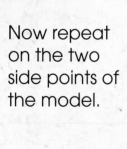

Now repeat on the two side points of the model.

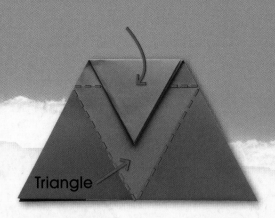

Triangle

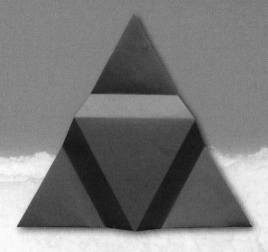

STEP 6:

Turn the model over. Fold down the top point of the model so the point touches the middle of the triangle in the center of the model, crease hard, and unfold.

Now repeat on the two side points of the model. Your model should now have six creases and look like this.

Pleat

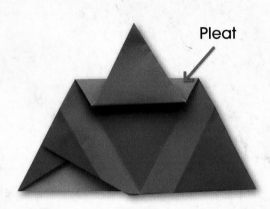

STEP 7:

Turn the model back over. Now using the creases you made in steps 5 and 6, create a pleat in the top point of the model. Then make a pleat with the left-hand point of the model.

Finally, make a pleat with the right-hand point of the model. Then tuck this pleat under one of the others to secure all three pleats.

Turn your star over, and it is complete!

Origami Hanukkah Wreath

Wreaths are a popular decoration during many holidays.

This Hanukkah, decorate your home with this fantastic wreath that's made completely from paper. You can use origami paper in white and shades of blue. You can also recycle gift-wrapping paper to add silver or patterned effects to your wreath.

The wreath is a modular model, which means it's made in small sections that are then slotted together. You can keep your wreath simple by just making the basic design, or decorate it with Hanukkah symbols such as the stars you made in the first project. Have fun!

To make a wreath, you will need:

Decorations for the wreath, such as paper Stars of David

8 sheets of paper in your choice of blue, white, or silver. Eight pieces of paper, each measuring 6 inches (15 cm) square, will make a wreath with a diameter of about 10 inches (25 cm).

Glue

(Origami paper is sometimes colored on both sides or white on one side.)

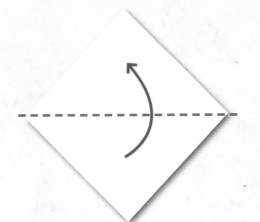

STEP 1:
Place the paper colored-side down, fold in half diagonally, and crease.

STEP 2:
Now fold up the right-hand point of the model, and crease hard.

STEP 3:
Then fold the top layer back down again along the dotted line, and crease hard.

13

STEP 4:

The right-hand point will have formed a small pocket. Gently open up the pocket and then carefully squash and flatten it back down so it forms a square.

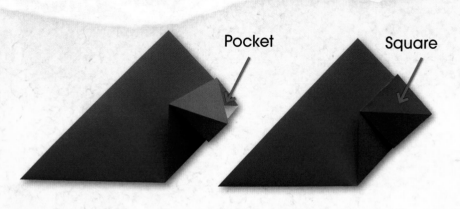

Pocket   Square

STEP 5:

Turn the model over. Fold down the top layer of paper along the dotted line, and crease.

STEP 6:

Fold in the right-hand point of the model, and crease hard.

STEP 7:

Turn the model back over, and your first module is complete. Repeat steps 1 to 6 with each of the other pieces of paper until you have eight modules in total.

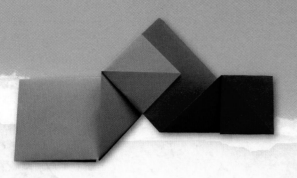

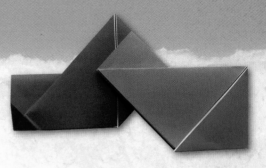

STEP 8:
Now take two modules and slot them together as shown.

Turn the model over and the two modules should look like this.

Now, folding along the dotted line, fold back the point of the light blue module so it tucks under and inside the part of the dark blue module directly beneath it.

Point

This fold will join the two modules, but for added security you can also tape or glue them together.

Keep joining the modules together, and finally attach module one to module eight to complete the wreath. Glue Stars of David or other decorations to your wreath.

Tealight Origami Menorah

Hanukkah is also known as the Festival of Lights. It celebrates a **miracle** that happened more than 2,000 years ago. At that time, the Jews were ruled by the Syrian-Greeks, who tried to force the Jews to give up their religion. The Jews fought back, and won. When they went to rededicate their temple by lighting the holy lamp, there was only enough oil for one day. The oil miraculously lasted for eight days, however, until more oil arrived.

During Hanukkah, Jews light candles every evening in a menorah. A menorah holds eight candles, one for each day of the miracle, and a ninth candle called the *shammash*, which is used to light the others. This year, using nine tealights and your paper folding skills, try making a simple origami menorah.

To make an origami tealight menorah, you will need:

18 squares of paper in your choice of white, silver, and shades of blue

9 tealight candles or 9 LED tealights

(Origami paper is sometimes colored on both sides or white on one side.)

STEP 1:

To make each candleholder, you will need two pieces of paper in different colors. Begin by placing one sheet of paper with the color you want facing up. We chose dark blue.

Fold the paper in half from side to side, crease, and unfold. Then fold up the bottom half of the paper, and crease.

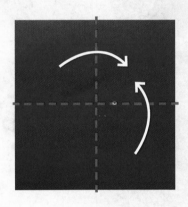

STEP 2:

Now fold the paper in half again, crease well, and then unfold.

STEP 3:

Now fold up the two bottom corners of the model so they meet the center crease, and crease hard.

STEP 4:

Now, folding only the top layer of paper, fold down the two top corners, and crease.

STEP 5:
Fold down the top flap of the model, and crease.

STEP 6:
Turn the model over, and it should look like this.

STEP 7:
Fold down the top half of the model, and crease. Your model should now look like this.

Now fold down the top two corners so they meet the center crease, and crease well.

STEP 8:
Fold the model in half, crease hard, and unfold. Then fold down the right-hand side of the model so it lines up with the center crease you've just made.

Next, fold down the left-hand side of the model.

Now unfold the two folds you've just made, and your model should look like this.

STEP 9:

Finally, gently open out the model along the long, top edge so it forms a boat shape. The creases you made in Step 8 will allow you to flatten the base of the candleholder so it sits flat on a tabletop.

STEP 10:

Now make a second boat-shaped section and sit one inside the other. The candleholder is now complete.

STEP 11:

Make another eight candleholders, add your candles or LED tealights, and your lights are ready to be arranged to create a menorah.

SAFETY ADVICE
Never leave your lighted tealight candles unattended.

Hanukkah Treats Basket

This next project shows you how to make cute origami baskets for serving candy, fruit and nuts, cookies, and other Hanukkah treats. A square of origami paper that's 6 inches (15 cm) square will make a small basket that measures about 2 inches (5 cm) across. Just right for a small serving of candy.

To make a basket, you will need:

Two sheets of paper in your choice of blue, white, or silver

Glue

Scissors

(Origami paper is sometimes colored on both sides or white on one side.)

STEP 1:

We chose to make a basket that's pale blue with dark blue patterns, so we began by placing the paper with the pale blue facing up.

Fold in half from side to side, crease, and then unfold. Fold in half from top to bottom, crease, and unfold.

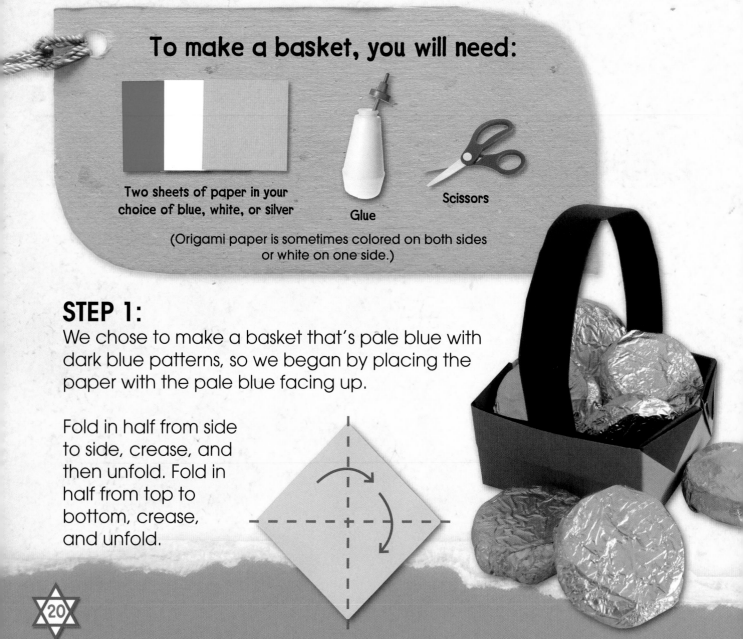

STEP 2:

Turn the paper over. Fold in half from side to side, crease, and then unfold. Fold in half from top to bottom, crease, and unfold.

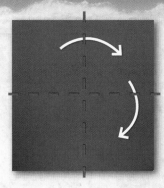

STEP 3:

Your piece of paper should now look like this.

Using the creases you made in Steps 1 and 2, fold up the paper by bringing point A in to meet point B, and point C down to meet point D.

Collapse and flatten the model to form a square.

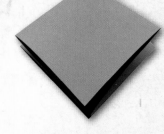

C

A   B

D

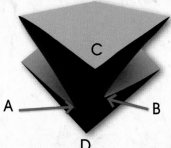

C

A   B

D

Open points

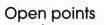

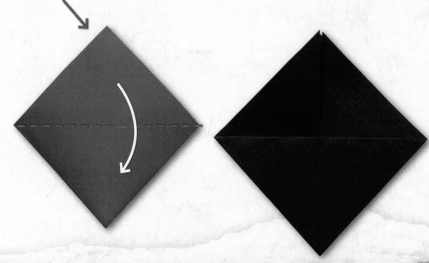

STEP 4:

Now turn the model 180 degrees so the open points are at the top. Then fold down the top layer of paper along the dotted line, and crease.

STEP 5:

Now fold the top layer of paper back up again so the bottom point meets the center of the model, and crease.

Then fold the top layer up one more time, and crease.

STEP 6:

Next, take hold of the right-hand point of the model, and working only with the top layer of paper, fold the right-hand side toward the left-hand side. Just like turning the page of a book.

Then fold the point back toward the right-hand side so it meets the center of the model, and crease.

Now fold the section of the model you've been working with back toward the right-hand side. Again, just like turning the page of a book.

Repeat everything in Step 6 on the left-hand side of the model.

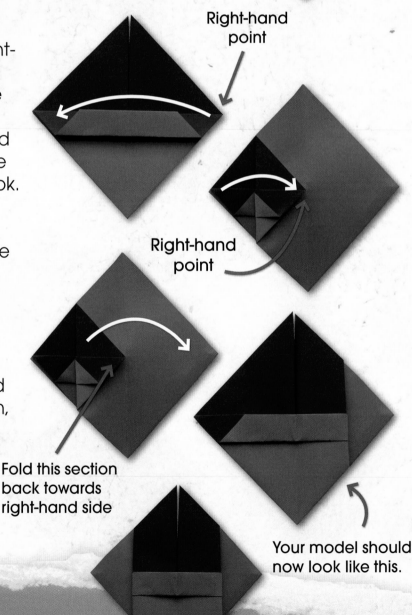

Right-hand point

Right-hand point

Fold this section back towards right-hand side

Your model should now look like this.

STEP 7:
Turn the model over and repeat steps 4 to 6. Your model should now look like this.

STEP 8:
Fold up the bottom of the model along the dotted line, crease hard, and unfold.

Now take hold of points A and B and gently pull them apart. The basket will start to pop open. Then you will carefully need to open out the base of the basket, flatten the bottom, and smooth out all the corners and edges.

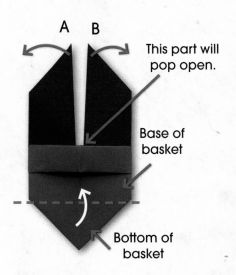

A B

This part will pop open.

Base of basket

Bottom of basket

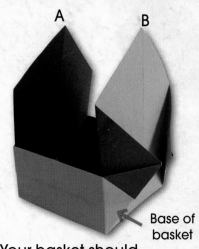

A   B

Base of basket

Your basket should now look like this.

STEP 9:
Fold down points A and B along the dotted lines, and tuck them neatly inside the basket. If you wish you can glue them in place.

STEP 10:
Finally, to make the basket's handle, cut a thick strip of paper from the second sheet. Fold it into three and glue the edge down.

Handle

Slot the ends of the handle into the sides of the basket and glue them in place.

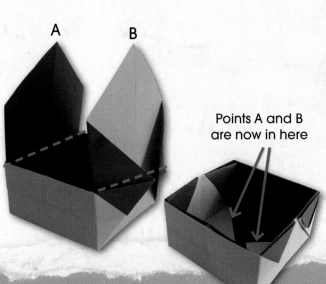

A   B

Points A and B are now in here

Origami Gift Box

Hanukkah is a time for giving gifts. So this year why not make pretty boxes for your gifts using your origami skills?

This next project shows you how to make a box with a lid. You can make miniboxes from squares of origami paper for small items such as jewelry or candy. Or make larger boxes from sheets of thick gift-wrapping paper. As long as you start with a square piece of paper, the design will work no matter the size of your paper.

Your friends and family will love receiving a Hanukkah gift in a handmade, **unique** gift box.

To make a box, you will need:

Two sheets of paper in your choice of colors
(one sheet should be slightly smaller then the other)

(Origami paper is sometimes colored on both sides or white on one side.)

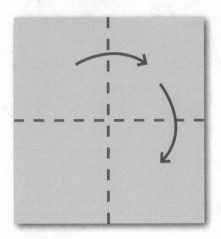

STEP 1:
Place the paper colored-side down. Fold in half from side to side, crease, and unfold. Fold in half from top to bottom, crease, and unfold.

STEP 2:
Now fold each of the four corners into the center of the model, and crease each edge well.

STEP 3:
Fold the top and the bottom of the model into the center, and crease hard.

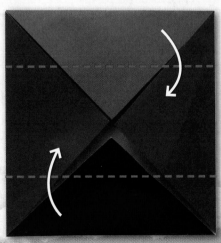

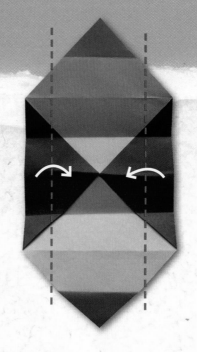

STEP 4:
Unfold the top and bottom points of the model and smooth them flat.

STEP 5:
Now fold the sides of the model into the center, and crease well.

STEP 6:
Fold the top of the model toward the left-hand along the dotted line, crease well, and unfold. Then repeat on the other side.

Then repeat this step on the bottom of the model.

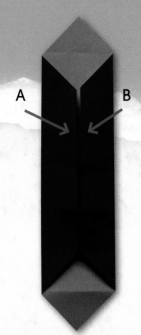

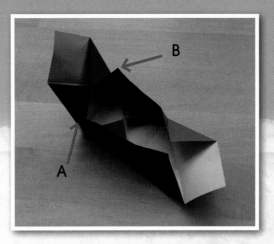

STEP 7:

Now take hold of points A and B and gently open them out. As you do this, the top of the model will rise up.

Fold the top point of the model inside the box and crease all the edges to shape the top edge of the box.

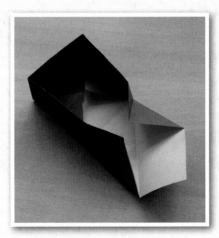

Repeat on the bottom of the model, and one half of your gift box is complete.

STEP 8:

Now take the second piece of paper and repeat all the steps to make the other half of the box.

Origami Gift Bow

In this final project, you will learn how to make a pretty paper bow that you can use to decorate a Hanukkah gift. You can make your bow from origami paper or recycled gift-wrapping paper.

You can even write a personal message in the center of your bow, to turn it into a bow and gift tag all in one. Have fun folding!

To make the origami bow, you will need:

Pen

One sheet of paper in your choice of color

(Origami paper is sometimes colored on both sides or white on one side.)

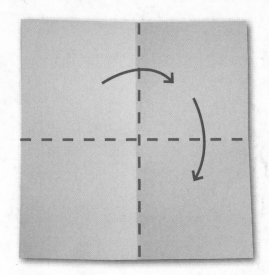

STEP 1:

Place the paper colored-side down. Fold in half from side to side, crease, and unfold. Fold in half from top to bottom, crease, and unfold.

Happy
Hanukkah

STEP 2:

In the center of the paper write a short Hanukkah message. The message can only fill about 1 square inch (2.5 sq cm) of paper.

STEP 3:

Now fold the four corners of the paper into the center and crease.

STEP 4:

Fold the four corners into the center of the model again, and crease well.

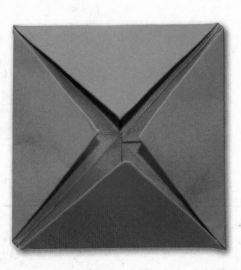

STEP 5:

Now fold the model's four corners into the center for a final time. The paper will be very thick, so crease hard.

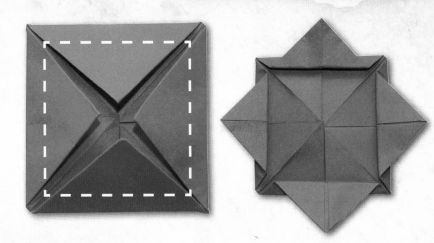

STEP 6:
Fold the four top flaps of the model back along the dotted lines, and crease well.

STEP 7:
Now fold the next four flaps that are inside the model back on themselves, and crease.

Happy Hanukkah

STEP 8:
Finally, fold the last four flaps in the center of the model back on themselves, and crease. Your message will now be revealed!

Glossary

emblem (EHM-blehm) A symbol used by a person or group of people as a means of identification.

miracle (MEER-uh-kul) An unexpected and favorable event that is not easily explained by science and that some may consider to be the work of a supreme being.

origami (or-uh-GAH-mee) The art of folding paper into decorative shapes or objects.

sculptures (SKULP-cherz) Works of art that have a shape to them, such as statues or carved objects, and may be made of wood, stone, metal, plaster, or even paper.

symbol (SIM-bul) Something that stands for or represents another thing, such as an important event or person. For example, a Star of David is a symbol of Judaism.

unique (yoo-NEEK) One of a kind.

Index

Websites

Due to the changing nature of Internet links, PowerKids Press has developed an online list of websites related to the subject of this book. This site is updated regularly. Please use this link to access the list: **www.powerkidslinks.com/ho/hanu**

Take heed, and bear witness
to the truths that lie within,
for they are the last legacy
of the Horadrim.

DIABLO

BOOK OF CAIN

Text by Flint Dille

INSIGHT EDITIONS

SAN RAFAEL, CALIFORNIA

My dear Leah,

In the inevitable event of my death, may I precede you by many decades to the grave.

Do not mourn me, Leah. Despite all I have been through, I have had a long and amazing life. I have died doing exactly what I was meant to do. I have lived and loved freely these long years—and have known only joy at seeing the bright, beautiful woman you've become. I believe that I now go on to a place beyond imagining, though I have no name for it, nor real understanding of where it lies, save beyond the broken bounds of this world.

I long for this paradise, Leah—and the peace and rest I might find there on the other side of this mortal existence. I want you to know this, dear one, above all other things I could have taught you— that there is hope beyond this reality, beyond the realms of Heaven and Hell and all the shadowed spaces that lie between. Hold fast to that hope in the face of the dark times ahead, and you will find the truest meaning of your life.

Though I know that you do not believe me when I speak of dread omens, I think you are beginning to suspect that my words ring of truth. I was a nonbeliever as well. I remember, even as a child, reading the Horadric tales and thinking that while they were wonderful stories, they were only that—wonderful stories. Tales such as those of Anu and the Dragon, the Mage Clan Wars, the Sin War, and the Hunt for the Three merely were told to embrace imagination. I now see, much to my regret, that even within these legends there lives a deeper and more profound truth. For, as I have come to discover, truth is hidden in unexpected places.

If events are as I believe them to be, some truths will be revealed very shortly which will make you a believer—perhaps even upon the day of my death. For I believe that if our world is to be saved, you have a pivotal role to play in its salvation, though I know not—nor do I begin to speculate—what that role might be.

Many of the things you will see in this book will be familiar to you. There are texts from the Great Library at Caldeum. I can never forget how, even as a young girl, you mastered the city. Although I was quite aware you were sneaking around the sewers (when you and I were not exploring old ruins), which led some to call me a negligent uncle. I further knew that the survival skills you would develop there, and likewise on the rest of our journeys, would prepare you for the work you have cut out for you. Here also you will find the drawings I made of the Neztem Petroglyphs, the strange mirrored cuneiform writings which I believe were made by one of the original nephalem. Much of this you will see again, but this time with the eyes of a Horadric scholar, not the eyes of a young girl. Understand this: As of my passing, you will become the last of the Horadrim.

At one time it had been my objective to write the first-ever history of the world, starting with the myth of Anu and the Dragon and continuing on to the events that unfold before us even as I write this letter. I use the example of the Stranger, who came to us so recently. It's becoming more and more clear who the Stranger in our midst truly is, and the sacrifice he must have made. Further, I have speculated on the true nature of the heroes who have also joined in our fight against the shadow. And most certainly you have done so as well.

Some material in here will be familiar to you from the dreams which have plagued you since childhood. Indeed, those dreams might be the key to preventing the end times.

Always, dear Leah, keep your eyes on the Prophecy. It is the key to the salvation of our world.

> . . . And, at the End of Days, Wisdom shall be lost
> as Justice falls upon the world of men.
> Valor shall turn to Wrath—
> and all Hope will be swallowed by Despair.
> Death, at last, shall spread its wings over all—
> as Fate lies shattered forever.

I cannot pretend that even I fully grasp how the knowledge contained herein informs the recent events in New Tristram, save only to say that we have already witnessed reawakened evils, and the mortal realm will see more before this is over. I must beg you, Leah, to stay vigilant and probe this book and, indeed, the people and lands you shall encounter. For within them, further glimpses of the truth shall be revealed to you.

The one thing I know is that the end times are not preordained. As I said, I believe there is something beyond all of this. I know not what, only that it exists. Jered Cain saw it, and, I am told, even Zoltun Kulle glimpsed it. Mark well this truth, though you do not yet believe that there is something far greater that awaits us outside all the suffering of this world. Sweet Leah, trust in your uncle until your doubts are removed.

Your first duty calls for you to forestall the end times. And now I must reveal to you that I, like you, have had prophetic dreams. In one such dream, not only did I see malefic forces at work, haunting echoes of the distant past—demons and angels—but, in the center of it all, I saw you standing between light and dark, between the Heavens and the Hells. The odd thing is that I had this dream of you when you were a child. However, in the dream you appeared just as you are now.

Study all that is written within these pages. All the work of my life, I now bequeath to you. I know not what in the writings is vital or what is offal. It is a compendium of knowledge collected throughout hundreds of years by adventurers, purveyors of dark arts, Horadric scholars, and madmen. Inside is information that will aid you in confronting the dark days that lie ahead. Do not mourn me, Leah. I have seen and heard accounts of those who have been beyond and returned. It is my belief that in death there are yet other mysteries to be revealed.

Live life well, my dear Leah.

All of my love,

Uncle Deckard

The Dawn

Anu and the Dragon

As with all things, it is best to begin with the beginning. The Creation. All things after it are a result of it, and the nature of it reverberates down through the millennia.

A great many mystic and tribal storytellers impart some version of this story. I am using ancient writings from the *Black Book of Lam Esen*. I choose this source because Lam Esen was a skilled sage renowned for his knowledge of Skatsimi mysticism and folklore. In his time, he collected vast stores of knowledge from diverse places, and had a unique genius for distilling the essence of things from a vast array of different sources.

He describes the creation of our universe in the following terms:

> *Before the beginning there was void. Nothing. No flesh. No rock.*
> *No air. No heat. No light. No dark.*
> *Nothing, save a single, perfect pearl.*
>
> *Within that pearl dreamed a mighty, unfathomable spirit—the One—Anu.*
> *Made of shining diamond, Anu was the sum of all things: good and evil,*
> *light and dark, physical and mystical, joy and sadness—all reflected across*
> *the crystalline facets of its form. And, within its eternal dream-state, Anu*
> *considered itself—all of its myriad facets. Seeking a state of total purity and*
> *perfection, Anu cast all evil from itself. All dissonance was gone. But what of*
> *the cast-off aspects of its being? The dark parts, the sharp, searing aspects of hate*
> *and pridefulness? Those could not remain in a state of separation, for all things*
> *are drawn to all things. All parts are drawn to the whole. Those discordant*
> *parts assembled into the Beast—the Dragon. Tathamet was his name—and he*
> *breathed unending death and darkness from his seven devouring heads. The*
> *Dragon was solely composed of Anu's cast-off aspects. The end sum of the*
> *whole became a singular Evil—the Prime Evil, from which all vileness would*
> *eventually spread throughout existence.*

Though separate beings, Anu and the Dragon were bound together within the Pearl's shadowed womb. There they warred against each other in an unending clash of light and shadow for ages uncounted.

The diamond warrior and the seven-headed dragon proved to be the equal of the other, neither ever gaining the upper hand in their fierce and unending combat—till at last, their energies nearly spent after countless millennia of battle, the two combatants delivered their final blows. The energies unleashed by their impossible fury ignited an explosion of light and matter so vast and terrible that it birthed the very universe all around us.

All of the stars above and the darkness that binds them.
All that we touch. All that we feel. All that we know.
All that is unknown.

All of it continues through the night and the day in the ebbing and flowing of the ocean tides and in the destruction of fire and the creation of the seed.

Everything of which we are aware, and that of which we are utterly unaware, was created with the deaths of Anu and the Dragon, Tathamet.

In the epicenter of reality lies Pandemonium, the scar of the universe's violent birth. At its chaotic center lay the Heart of Creation, a massive jewel unlike any other: the Eye of Anu—the Worldstone. It is the foundation stone of all places and times, a nexus of realities and vast, untold possibility.

Anu and Tathamet are no more, yet their distinct essences permeated the nascent universe—and eventually became the bedrock of what we know to be the High Heavens and the Burning Hells.

Anu's shining spine spun out into the primordial darkness, where it slowed and cooled. Over countless ages it formed into the Crystal Arch, around which the High Heavens took shape and form.

Though Anu was gone, some resonance of it remained in the holy Arch. Spirits bled forth from it—shining angels of light and sound who embodied the virtuous aspects of what the One had been.

Yet, despite the grace and beauty of this shining realm, it lacked the perfection of Anu's spirit. Anu had passed into a benevolent place beyond this broken universe—a paradise of which nothing is known, and yet represents perhaps the greatest-kept secret of Creation.

Longed for, but unimaginable.

Just as Heaven cooled in the spaces above, Tathamet's blackened, smoldering husk spiraled into the lower darkness of reality. From his putrid flesh grew the realms of the Burning Hells. The Dragon's seven severed heads arose as the seven Evils—the three strongest of which would be known as the Prime Evils. They, along with their four Lesser brethren, would rule over the ravening, demonic hordes that spawned like maggots from the desiccated cavities of the Burning Hells.

Thus was how all of what we know began . . . In time, the Lords of Hell and the angels of Heaven met and clashed. The battle raged unceasing, and thus would come to be known as the Eternal Conflict. It is written in the Book of Long Shadows that the Eternal Conflict shall continue on forever across countless planes of existence, until further mysteries, unknown even to the angels and the demons, shall reveal themselves.

Over the millennia, many scholars have interpreted this in various ways. Some, especially in the primitive tribes who look to the sky for their understanding of the universe, view all this as literally true. They believe that Anu's spine is a physical object in the universe. That demons are born from the rotting flesh of Tathamet.

Other scholars and mystics take this less literally and perceive the telling of Anu and Tathamet's battle as an elaborate metaphor for good and evil and the constant, warring dynamic seen among the forces of nature.

The Eternal Conflict

I take the following knowledge from a surviving fragment of one of the scrolls of the Church of Zakarum. In it, the unknown scribe tells of events which took place millennia before the founding of the church. Thus, the descriptions are of questionable validity. I personally believe that the tales came from earlier and unknown sources. I have my suspicions, which, for the time, I will keep to myself—although I might expatiate on these things in a later writing. The scroll describes a war fought by agents of light and order against creatures of chaos and shadow. That is to say, forces both of the High Heavens and the Burning Hells (see later sections).

This war was most commonly fought within the realm of Pandemonium. According to one of the earliest necromancers, the angels and demons battled over control of one essential object, the Heart of Creation—the Worldstone.

The Worldstone is not, as the name implies, a mere stone. It is a colossal, mountain-sized object which was believed by many (and is supported by multiple petroglyphs and ancient sculptures) to be the actual Eye of Anu, the One. According to legend, to which I subscribe, the Worldstone is an artifact of unimaginable power.

Lacking the specificity and background a scholar such as I would like, a belief exists that control of this stone changed hands many times over the eons. Oral history tells us that the Worldstone *"allowed the side that possessed it to alter reality and create life and worlds almost without restriction."* The account continues that *"angels used the stone to build worlds of perfect order in line with their ideals of justice, hope, wisdom, fate, and valor,"* whereas demons used the stone to *"create unfathomable engines of annihilation and worlds of destruction, terror, and hatred. However, these worlds created by angels and demons never flourished. They were inherently flawed, and doomed to wither and die."*

I know not whether such worlds were ever created or, if they were, whether any of them still exist. To the best of my knowledge, no man has ever beheld such a world. Therefore, I suspect that this account is literary license. What we can all agree upon, however, is that this object was of great importance and that, whatever its use, it was greatly coveted by the angels and demons.

Further research suggests that in time, an archangel called Tyrael ordered a bastion to be built around the Worldstone, a stronghold which would come to be known as the Pandemonium Fortress. Throughout these writings, I will explore much further the tales surrounding Tyrael, as I have, indeed, actually met the angel.

Read these sections carefully, my dear. Read all things about him carefully, for if my suspicions are correct, he still has some role to play in this grand drama.

I can testify to the existence of the Pandemonium Fortress, as I was once there. I can tell you from firsthand experience that this stronghold embodies the warped-reality traits ascribed to Pandemonium as a whole. Indeed, I have never seen anything quite like it. That having been said, I cannot be sure whether it is simply otherworldly in nature or it was built by an angel or a mad demon. In any case, over the course of the Eternal Conflict, the fortress changed hands between angels and demons. Thus, it has taken on structural and metaphysical traits from both the High Heavens and the Burning Hells.

Long ago, an angel known as Inarius seized the Worldstone and, through some impossible act of magic, veiled it from the sight of both Heaven and Hell. He had accomplished this with the aid, I presume, of the mysterious demoness Lilith and a cadre of other angels and demons who had grown disillusioned with the Eternal Conflict. Inarius succeeded in manipulating the power of the stone to create the world of Sanctuary, a hidden paradise where he and his followers could live free from the madness of unending strife.

This is the place we know as the mortal realm. This is our world. We must pause a moment to think upon this. Our world, unlike all the other worlds, was created by both angels and demons.

The day of Sanctuary's creation, the nature of the Eternal Conflict changed. Much confusion spread through the Burning Hells and the High Heavens. The center of all things they had fought over for countless millennia had vanished. It was simply gone. At first both sides suspected the other, but in time, they realized that the truth was something different. Thus it was that the battle for possession of the Worldstone became the search for it.

It is interesting to note, before we begin delving into the Burning Hells and High Heavens, that not all things assumed of them are true.

For instance, there were different cults which reigned in the period between what we now know as the Sin War and the Dark Exile (both of which I will discuss later). It was believed by some that the High Heavens and the Burning Hells were places where the souls of men went when they died—that men either were rewarded for their virtues (the High Heavens), or received punishment for their failings (the Burning Hells). Aside from the unfounded beliefs of various cults, there is nothing in academia to support this. It is important that the reader understand that the High Heavens and the Burning Hells, much like the realm of Pandemonium, are actual, physical locations in this universe.

Personally, I believe that there exists a place where the souls of men go after their death, but that discussion is beyond the place of this treatise.

This being said, I must confess that even I do not always know where myth ends and truth begins. That, reader, I will let you judge for yourself.

The Burning Hells
Realms of Evil

As to the nature of the demons of Hell, I can testify only to having personally seen Diablo and other manner of terrors in both Tristram and elsewhere on Sanctuary, but my experiences are nonetheless limited in the broad scheme of things. I must defer to other sources, such as the writings of Vischar Orous, chief librarian for the Zharesh Covenant, a small offshoot of the notorious Vizjerei mage clan. Orous' careful and scholarly research of the Prime Evils and other demons has been passed to us through historical and scientific tomes.

One intriguing piece of information I have gleaned from Orous' research is that not all abominations and violations that appear in Sanctuary are of hellish or demonic origin. For instance, the walking dead are unique to Sanctuary and are not created in the Burning Hells, but they can be awakened from their morbid sleep by activities of demons and angels.

In other areas I have turned to the writings of my own ancestor, Jered Cain, for information, especially as it concerns the Prime Evils he and his brother mages battled.

The accounts by man of the Burning Hells are very limited. (I myself have gone only so far as the Pandemonium Fortress.) Orous relies on information gained by Vizjerei mages who summoned demons into Sanctuary and interrogated them in most ingenious ways. Other information has been gained by casting holy powers into possessed humans, compelling demons who reside within them to speak.

"Seven is the number of the powers of Hell, and seven is the number of the Great Evils."

— Vischar Orous

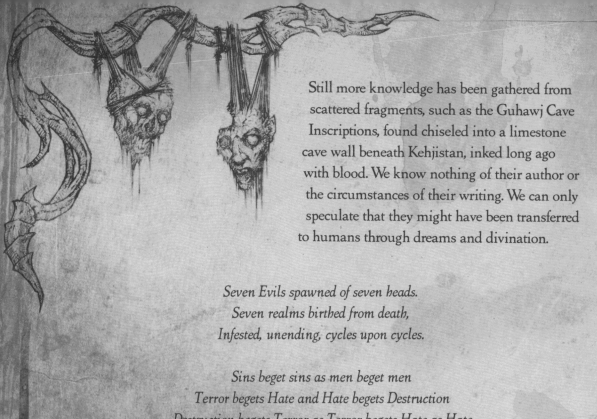

Still more knowledge has been gathered from scattered fragments, such as the Guhawj Cave Inscriptions, found chiseled into a limestone cave wall beneath Kehjistan, inked long ago with blood. We know nothing of their author or the circumstances of their writing. We can only speculate that they might have been transferred to humans through dreams and divination.

Seven Evils spawned of seven heads.
Seven realms birthed from death,
Infested, unending, cycles upon cycles.

Sins beget sins as men beget men
Terror begets Hate and Hate begets Destruction
Destruction begets Terror as Terror begets Hate as Hate
begets Destruction as Destruction begets . . .

(The inscription is unreadable from this point, but it has been speculated that this incantation repeats many times.)

The Neztem Petroglyphs

The Neztem Petroglyphs were found on what is believed to be a natural pillar far out in the deserts of Aranoch. As a personal note and observation, my young ward, Leah, was with me on this journey. Upon staring at this rock, she began having visions of a most violent nature. I had to confine her to the tent for the rest of our time there. I have used some of what she said during those visions to inform my descriptions of Hell in the following section.

The Prime Evils

THE LORDS OF THE BURNING HELLS

Mark well the words that follow, and let them serve as a warning to all men of what the Lords of the Burning Hells may have planned for the future of Sanctuary should they ever invade our realm.

Let it be known that there exists a hierarchy to the Hells.
There are three Prime Evils and four Lesser Evils.

The Prime Evils are Diablo, Lord of Terror; Baal, Lord of Destruction; and Mephisto, Lord of Hatred. These Prime Evils are brothers—it is said that they were the dominant heads of the Dragon, Tathamet. These three Evils endeavor to maintain a strict rule over the Hells' legions. As the Guhawj Cave poem indicates, these powers fuel each other. Terror leads to Hatred, and Hatred leads to Destruction. This has allowed them to be the dominant force of Hell in such a way that they generate energy that has been analogized to an alchemist's engine.

The Lesser Evils are four in number. The first is Andariel, the Maiden of Anguish. Andariel is the twin sister of Duriel, a male Evil who is referred to as the Lord of Pain. The final two Evils are the ones most mysterious to us, for they have not yet come to Sanctuary. However, many of the prophecies express a fear that they will. These two are Belial, Lord of Lies, and Azmodan, Lord of Sin.

As we have now briefly introduced the hierarchy of Hell, it is time to explore each individually. We shall focus also upon what is known of the Evils' domains in Hell. It is interesting to note here that the borders of their domains are constantly shifting as the boundaries within the Hells crash into and encroach upon one another. Judging by the texts and accounts, it is as if the borders themselves are in conflict.

Let us not dwell overlong on these horrors, however, lest we ourselves sink into the depths of madness.

DIABLO, THE LORD OF TERROR

Of all of the Great Evils, it is much to our misfortune that we know the most about the Lord of Terror, Al'Diabolos, known more widely as Diablo.

He is the root of all fears buried deep within mortal minds. He is the nightmare that awakens us, sweating in the dark. He is an entity of pure malevolence and depthless evil. He has plagued Sanctuary on several occasions and tormented mortals time and again, more often than any of his foul brethren.

Despite the fact that age as we know it does not seem to apply to the Lords of Hell, Diablo is generally considered to be the youngest of the Three. It may also seem odd to assign positive traits to a demon; nonetheless, it is said that Diablo is the most creative and farsighted of his brothers, perhaps of all of the Evils. Many claim that Mephisto is the most intelligent, but intelligence has as many facets as does evil.

Diablo is calm, cunning, and patient, and best understood when we view all his actions as attempts to instill terror in those around him. Consider the components of terror: a mix of fear, shock, and utter hopelessness. Perhaps Diablo's most insidious power is the ability to cast his influence deep in the minds of his victims and latch upon their greatest, most crippling fears, then to apply that knowledge and, in so doing, use a person's own worst fears against them.

As perverse as it may sound, Diablo sees himself as an artist of terror. I can attest that when I was subjected to Diablo's evil, it seemed to me as if he derived from it the pleasure that an artist takes in his work. Perhaps he sees each of us as a canvas.

Diablo knows that conquest comes when enemies panic and turn their backs to their fears, rather than face them. However—and this is an important concept to grasp—Diablo does not acquire his satisfaction from conquest itself, as perhaps Mephisto might. Diablo feeds on the terror that precedes the conquest. To him, the fear a victim has is a greater reward than the pain they suffer when they are actually tortured.

With this perspective on Diablo's nature, it remains now for us to describe his Realm of Terror within the Burning Hells.

Vischar Orous states, from the extracted testimony of demons who claim to be familiar with this realm of living nightmare, that it is the least populated of all the territories of Hell, for few demons can withstand its unrelenting torment.

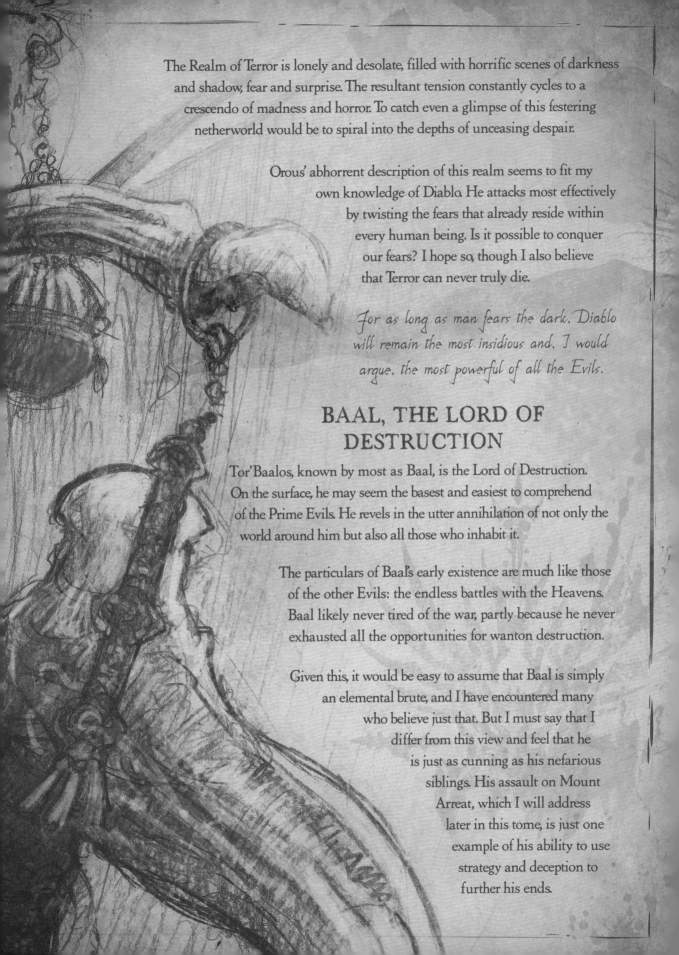

The Realm of Terror is lonely and desolate, filled with horrific scenes of darkness and shadow, fear and surprise. The resultant tension constantly cycles to a crescendo of madness and horror. To catch even a glimpse of this festering netherworld would be to spiral into the depths of unceasing despair.

Orous' abhorrent description of this realm seems to fit my own knowledge of Diablo. He attacks most effectively by twisting the fears that already reside within every human being. Is it possible to conquer our fears? I hope so, though I also believe that Terror can never truly die.

For as long as man fears the dark, Diablo will remain the most insidious and, I would argue, the most powerful of all the Evils.

BAAL, THE LORD OF DESTRUCTION

Tor'Baalos, known by most as Baal, is the Lord of Destruction. On the surface, he may seem the basest and easiest to comprehend of the Prime Evils. He revels in the utter annihilation of not only the world around him but also all those who inhabit it.

The particulars of Baal's early existence are much like those of the other Evils: the endless battles with the Heavens. Baal likely never tired of the war, partly because he never exhausted all the opportunities for wanton destruction.

Given this, it would be easy to assume that Baal is simply an elemental brute, and I have encountered many who believe just that. But I must say that I differ from this view and feel that he is just as cunning as his nefarious siblings. His assault on Mount Arreat, which I will address later in this tome, is just one example of his ability to use strategy and deception to further his ends.

By all accounts, Baal's realm in the Burning Hells is a frenzy of constant destruction wherein he breeds demons only for the sheer gratification of destroying them. It is said that he has built some of the mightiest structures in the Hells, perfecting bastions of impenetrable strength, only to see them pulverized in unique and different ways.

There is one other thing of great import to remember.

At the heart of the Realm of Destruction lies the Hellforge, which, ironically, is the realm's single source of creation. This is one of the very few places in Hell men have actually seen, and those who have been there have reported that the greatest weapons of the Burning Hells are forged within it.

It is said that Hellforged weapons are infused with elements of the Lords of Hell. Of course, it must also be noted that these items are used to destroy. Once again, we see that the theme of creation and destruction rings through all things associated with Baal.

MEPHISTO, THE LORD OF HATRED

Dul'Mephistos, known commonly as Mephisto, is the Lord of Hatred. There are some who believe that if there is truly a leader among the Burning Hells, it is Mephisto.

It has been said also that Mephisto is the most adept at playing his brothers against each other. Diablo and Baal chafe at his manipulations, but more often than not they comply, most likely because Mephisto provides them with ample opportunities to pursue their ambitions. Perhaps this is why Mephisto is seen by some to be a unifier, a great tactician.

It is Mephisto's greatest ambition to pit entire societies against one another, to turn brother against brother, sowing discord and distrust at every turn. The Lord of Hatred might look at Sanctuary as his own private ant farm, presenting him with endless, fascinating opportunities to fuel the flames of conflict.

To Mephisto, hatred is a tool, though one he wields with utmost precision. The Lord of Hatred despises all, but he loathes angels above all else. And so the inhabitants of Sanctuary are seen by him as weapons to be forged in his likeness, to be aimed one day at the High Heavens.

And if history is any indication, Mephisto is well positioned, for hatred has shaped more of humankind's history than all the other evils combined.

It would be wise to note here that bards and chroniclers alike have stated that Mephisto is the father of two demons, Lucion and Lilith.

The Hellforge is said to consist of many anvils, including the Anvil of Annihilation. Yeah, see my writings in "The Dark Wanderer."

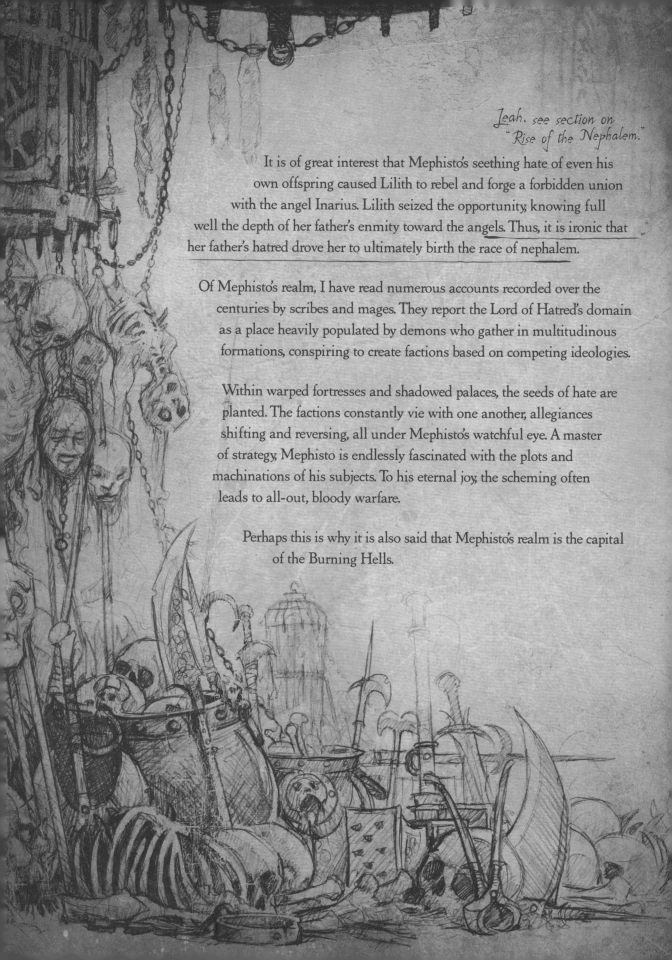

Leah, see section on "Rise of the Nephalem."

It is of great interest that Mephisto's seething hate of even his own offspring caused Lilith to rebel and forge a forbidden union with the angel Inarius. Lilith seized the opportunity, knowing full well the depth of her father's enmity toward the angels. Thus, it is ironic that her father's hatred drove her to ultimately birth the race of nephalem.

Of Mephisto's realm, I have read numerous accounts recorded over the centuries by scribes and mages. They report the Lord of Hatred's domain as a place heavily populated by demons who gather in multitudinous formations, conspiring to create factions based on competing ideologies.

Within warped fortresses and shadowed palaces, the seeds of hate are planted. The factions constantly vie with one another, allegiances shifting and reversing, all under Mephisto's watchful eye. A master of strategy, Mephisto is endlessly fascinated with the plots and machinations of his subjects. To his eternal joy, the scheming often leads to all-out, bloody warfare.

Perhaps this is why it is also said that Mephisto's realm is the capital of the Burning Hells.

The Lesser Evils

Compared to the Primes, there is much less knowledge to be found regarding the Lesser Evils. Only two of the four—Andariel and Duriel—have ever been seen in the mortal realm. The other two, Belial and Azmodan, are known only by secondhand account. It is these latter two who I fear might bring about the end times.

Dear reader, do not be fooled by the designation of "Prime" or "Lesser": It is one that is relevant only within the Burning Hells and does not mean that one Evil is more or less dangerous to us mortals.

In fact, it is probable that the Lesser Evils are more dangerous than the Primes. It is, after all, known that the four Lesser Evils rose up against the Primes and banished them to Sanctuary in a rebellion termed the Dark Exile. *detailed elsewhere in this volume*

I will start first with the Lesser Evils who are known to us. Duriel and Andariel are what men would wrongly call fraternal twins; in the realm of demons, their intimate relationship seems to have more to do with their corresponding spheres of pain and anguish than with any actual blood connection.

DURIEL, THE LORD OF PAIN

Duriel, brother to Andariel, is also known as the Maggot King, or the Lord of Pain. He has been seen only once on Sanctuary, in the form of a horrific, grotesque maggot-like aberration.

By all accounts, Duriel loves to torture and inflict pain. The bizarre thing, which I think is not fully comprehensible to us mortals, is that he doesn't seem to care what the pain means to the recipient. He appears to love the music of the screams: the disharmony of agony at a sensual level. He thinks of himself as a maestro of pain. He is interested not in mental anguish but in physical torment.

Many writings suggest that if Duriel is in a position where there is no victim for him to inflict torture upon, he will subject himself to excruciating pain and be sated.

Ironically, given how little is known of the Lesser Evil himself, Duriel's place in the Burning Hells is the one most widely chronicled in the ancient artworks. I suspect that this is because it most closely resembles the torture chambers of our own realm and therefore is most easily understood and depicted by human artists and writers.

The Realm of Pain is described as a cavernous area fitted with increasingly sadistic and grotesque torture devices, from towering machines that house unspeakable engines of brutality to tiny mechanisms engineered to elicit agony beyond imagining. Here Duriel derives exquisite gratification from the torment of thousands of captive, barbarous demons. It is said that even the other denizens of Hell, including his sister, whose realm in some perverse way overlaps his, avoid this place, though they delight in the music of agonized screams that issues from it.

ANDARIEL, THE MAIDEN OF ANGUISH

Andariel, known as the Maiden of Anguish, is a particularly sadistic entity. Unlike her so-called twin, Duriel, she is interested not in physical pain but in emotional agony. She believes in the purity of anguish.

She is a master manipulator who sets up scenarios in which the victim's mental state is twisted inside out. She loves seeing people torn apart by their own inner agony and emotional pain. The Maiden of Anguish was once considered a close confidante of Diablo—until the Dark Exile, that is, when she and her companions ruthlessly betrayed him. Despite their former allegiance, she reveled in Diablo's misery and was described as enjoying a state of unmatched bliss throughout his humiliating defeat. Her general bearing is of one who is in a constant state of ecstasy, experiencing unthinkable pleasures. Andariel, considered one of the most relation oriented of the Evils, is said to abhor isolation, for she sustains herself on the suffering of others. She is drawn to conflict and tragedy as a moth to flame. She seems to be in constant motion, seeking those in the depths of despair, or those most susceptible to her influence and manipulation.

There is little information on what her realm in the Burning Hells is like, but clearly it is a place of psychological assault, where guilt, regret, and self-loathing are meted out through both physical and mental means.

It has been suggested that the victims of Andariel's realm, crippled by guilt and driven to seek unending physical torment, willingly give themselves over to Duriel's domain.

AZMODAN, THE LORD OF SIN

Azmodan, Lord of Sin, is a clever manipulator who trades in vice and corruption. He is passionate and plotting—both to very dangerous degrees. He is by far the most charismatic and seductive of all the Evils.

Azmodan takes pleasure in all things to every possible extreme. He loves vice in all its forms, but the truest gratification he derives is from the failures of others. Azmodan is a master of temptation, of causing those who hold steadfastly to principles and beliefs to ultimately betray them. Azmodan can see most clearly the heart's desires. He exists only to shred morality, to bring any and all within his sphere to the point of breaking.

Perhaps if one could analyze the inner workings of Azmodan, they would see that the Lord of Sin defines the universe through the extremes that one is willing to go to; he believes that all beings find their truest identity by embracing the far limits of perversion and depravity.

If this is difficult for the reader to grasp, do not feel stymied. There are scholars and sages who have meditated on and contemplated this subject for years, and still wrestle with their understanding.

We are a race of joy and nurturing that is tainted and tempted by sin, but rare is the human who sets out to commit sin; sin is a web we are drawn into.

Azmodan would surely find fertile ground on Sanctuary to plant the seeds of corruption, but fortunately he has never, to the best of my knowledge, appeared upon the mortal plane.

It is said in the scrolls of Malzakam that Azmodan's land in the Hells is the most densely populated—that it is a warped arena of myriad sins, of both great joy and despair, a place where garish perversions are indulged to the extreme.

The scrolls also suggest that Azmodan's den at first does not appear fearsome or disgusting, but rather looks to be a seductive warren that leads downward and downward through an increasingly labyrinthine harem. Here, sated to revulsion with all the pleasures of life, one descends rapidly into a perverse madness, without any hope of awakening one's rotted soul.

Much like the provocative hymns sung by pleasure maidens in Lut Gholein, the Malzakam scrolls infer that pleasure, when imbibed too freely or when prolonged for too great a time, becomes indistinguishable from pain. Conversely, at certain levels, pain itself becomes pleasure.

While I understand the theory, I have no interest in experiencing it firsthand. I believe, as the scrolls attest, that those who would embrace sin will quickly become lost with no hope of return.

May the Heavens help us if Azmodan should ever arrive upon the mortal plane.

BELIAL, THE LORD OF LIES

Once again, I have no firsthand knowledge of Belial. What I do know is that the Lord of Lies is depicted in various writings as a trickster and master deceiver.

Belial advocates the notion that perception is reality, and it is his sole purpose to dominate reality. He does not lie simply for the sake of lying; rather, he deceives with the overall intent of controlling others' perception of what is real.

The Lord of Lies relishes the moment his victim realizes he's been deceived, that moment of nakedness and betrayal. It is my feeling that should we encounter him on this plane, he would appear as a master orator, a mortal of immense influence and means, perhaps even a respected leader. Beneath this facade would lurk the true Belial—covert, wicked, and brilliant, a creature of great clarity and deftness. He would hatch plots within plots and drive humankind to ruin.

Should there be an invasion of the mortal realm, expect deception to cloak it. Belial's weakness, perhaps, is that his deception does not stop with others, for he is often trapped within the intricate webs of his own machinations.

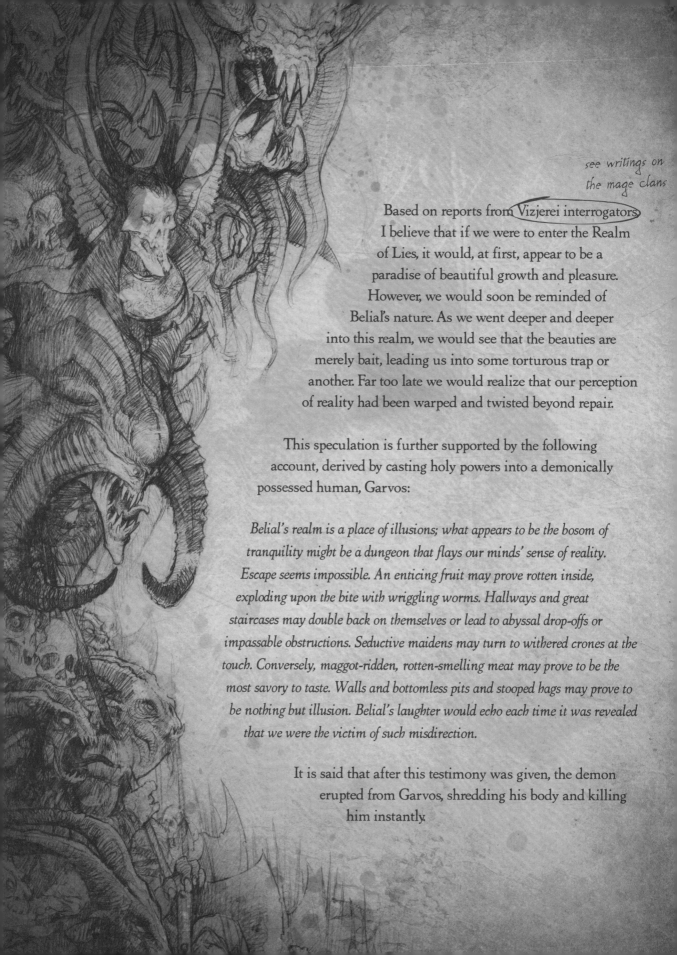

see writings on
the mage clans

Based on reports from Vizjerei interrogators
I believe that if we were to enter the Realm
of Lies, it would, at first, appear to be a
paradise of beautiful growth and pleasure.
However, we would soon be reminded of
Belial's nature. As we went deeper and deeper
into this realm, we would see that the beauties are
merely bait, leading us into some torturous trap or
another. Far too late we would realize that our perception
of reality had been warped and twisted beyond repair.

This speculation is further supported by the following
account, derived by casting holy powers into a demonically
possessed human, Garvos:

*Belial's realm is a place of illusions; what appears to be the bosom of
tranquility might be a dungeon that flays our minds' sense of reality.
Escape seems impossible. An enticing fruit may prove rotten inside,
exploding upon the bite with wriggling worms. Hallways and great
staircases may double back on themselves or lead to abyssal drop-offs or
impassable obstructions. Seductive maidens may turn to withered crones at the
touch. Conversely, maggot-ridden, rotten-smelling meat may prove to be the
most savory to taste. Walls and bottomless pits and stooped hags may prove to
be nothing but illusion. Belial's laughter would echo each time it was revealed
that we were the victim of such misdirection.*

It is said that after this testimony was given, the demon
erupted from Garvos, shredding his body and killing
him instantly.

Conclusions

In closing, we should not, for even a moment, believe that because the Lesser Evils are referred to as such that we can relax our guard, for as I have said, the so-called Lesser Evils are every bit as dangerous and ingenious as the Primes, and perhaps more so, because we have had very little direct interaction with them. Remember also the omens that foretell a time of great sin and deception across the mortal world. These signs may be the harbingers of our doom.

"Man's pleasures give way to pain. His truths are buried in the shroud of lies.

It is this time when Hell shall reign. While all of man dies."

This is clearly an indication that Belial and Azmodan may even now be on the move. It is imperative that we not develop a false sense of confidence when we consider the combative nature of these Evils toward one another. It must always be remembered that they work together as well when it suits their interests.

We must therefore be on our guard against the coming predations of Belial and Azmodan.

The High Heavens
The Angiris Council

A s with the Burning Hells, I personally have never ventured to the High Heavens. However, I have met the archangel Tyrael and, thereby, know angels to exist. I further have acquired some knowledge of their powers. Much of what follows is derived from recovered texts written by the Horadrim during the Hunt for the Three. These texts were assembled in the monastery built by the Horadrim at Tristram, where the order settled after capturing the three Prime Evils. These writings may well shine a light on the High Heavens and all the wonders that one might behold there, including the Angiris Council, the ruling body of the Heavens.

The reader should understand that these manuscripts are supported by many other artifacts I have either collected or observed in my travels about the world. I do not demand the reader believe my word alone.

To many scholars, the archangels of the Angiris Council are living representations of the chief virtues of Anu. It is important that we understand that these beings are not like men. They are not made of flesh and blood. They do not age and die as we do.

In their pure existence, angels are of a divine essence of light and sound. Radiance marked with beautiful harmony. Although the reader may find this description abstract, I believe that angels in the High Heavens exist more like magnificent movements of music and light. It is told that even the armor the angels wear is ornamental and used more to provide a sense of individuality than to protect. It is written that the angels have worn this armor since the beginning, long before the appearance of humankind, so their use of it is certainly not an attempt to appear more like humans. I believe the armor to be both functional and decorative, though I must admit this is merely supposition on my part.

It is the angels' majestic wings of light that speak of their truest manifestation. Angels are a magnificent sight to behold, appearing as mortals, but at the same time looking utterly otherworldly. Whatever the case, it is important that you know angels do exist. They have been known to take great interest in the affairs on our world, just as demons do. It should also be noted that much of this interest comes from fear, for they believe that we humans hold great untapped power within us. A power perhaps greater than that of the angels themselves.

This is our nephalem birthright—but I am getting ahead of myself; the nature of our extraordinary heritage will be discussed later.

For now, in order to gain a greater understanding of the angels, it is necessary that we discuss the members of the Angiris Council one by one. I will begin by describing each, as well as the legendary items they wield.

IMPERIUS, ARCHANGEL OF VALOR

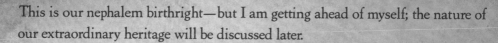

Imperius is the leader of the Angiris Council, if leadership exists at all in the human sense. It is he who commands the warrior host of the High Heavens. His tactical brilliance encompasses all facets of warfare, from maneuvering armies on the battlefields to leading covert strikes against Hell's outposts.

Over the long eons of the Eternal Conflict, Imperius has tread where other angels do not dare. When the great war has turned in Heaven's favor, he has been the first to spearhead the most daring assaults into the heart of the Burning Hells.

Even in the face of defeat, Imperius' bravery is unshakable. When Hell's legions lay siege to the High Heavens, it is Imperius who rallies his fellow angels to action. He is the first to storm out of the Diamond Gates and charge headlong into the scattering armies of the Hells. The mere sight of Imperius in action emboldens the angels with valor and strength.

In speaking of Imperius' exploits, I must also mention Solarion, the Spear of Valor. Legend tells that the archangel forged this weapon in the heart of a dying star. I have heard it described as an extension of his immutable will, powerful enough to sunder Hell's mightiest ramparts with a single righteous strike. During one of Imperius' invasions of the Burning Hells, it is written that Solarion felled so many demons that rivers of blood flowed throughout the realms of the seven Evils.

I should note here that Imperius does not carry the spear at his side at all times. Rather, he summons it from on high as a lance of blinding light that then manifests as a physical spear in his hand.

When not clashing with Hell's minions, Imperius often strategizes, and trains other warrior angels in the Halls of Valor, his place in the High Heavens. Skatsimi mystics describe the archangel's domain as a series of vast, glowing chambers that echo with songs of his valorous deeds. There, his trophies of war are displayed in perpetuity.

If we take the above to be true, then undoubtedly, Imperius must be held in high regard for his leadership and martial prowess. However, his legendary valor appears to come with the fatal flaw of pride. It is this pride and arrogance which have reportedly brought him into conflict with Tyrael, the archangel of Justice. This is due in large part to the pact that Tyrael helped make between the Heavens and the Hells at the conclusion of the Sin War (an event I will discuss in

depth later). The treaty brought the Eternal Conflict to a grinding halt, thus robbing Imperius of further opportunities to prove his valor in combat.

Since that time (and surely due in no small part to the later actions of Tyrael, as we shall see), it is said that Imperius has become a highly legalistic and unbending tyrant. Although it is likely not his intent, Imperius' obstinacy has allegedly caused disharmony to creep into the Angiris Council.

TYRAEL, ARCHANGEL OF JUSTICE

The only member of the Angiris Council I have seen with my own eyes is Tyrael, the archangel of Justice. I might even say I know him, if it is truly possible to know an angel.

Ages before the rise of man, it is said Tyrael was the most rigid of the angels, firm in his adherence to laws, rules, and order. He held to a single, unbending duty: to secure victory for the High Heavens in the Eternal Conflict.

As with Imperius, Tyrael's exploits in battle are the stuff of legend. He was renowned for being calm and controlled and meticulous in his execution of combat technique. The archangel carried out his impassive judgment through the use of El'druin, the Sword of Justice.

El'druin is, by all accounts, a unique weapon that can cut through any substance or foe in existence. There is, however, an exception: Some believe that the blade's edge cannot pass through or harm any being of righteous intent.

Despite Tyrael's fame as a warrior with few peers, it is nonetheless stated that he was at all times fair and impartial, as justice itself must be.

The Courts of Justice, Tyrael's abode in the High Heavens, are said to be akin to a great auditorium wherein angels congregate. Here they air grievances, come to terms, and strive to reclaim lost harmony or equilibrium. It seems a fitting institution for an angel who values integrity and balance above all things, and will choose the path of righteousness in any situation, even if it brings harm to those he loves.

In light of all that is stated above, it is ironic that Tyrael is now considered to be the renegade of the Angiris Council. Much of this is due to the fact that since the appearance of mortals, Tyrael has evidenced a change of character. He has intervened for the sake of humankind time and again, for he sees the potential for heroism and selflessness in each of us. He has even acted against the mandates of his fellow Council members to fight on our behalf.

For that alone I always have and always will believe in him.

I will discuss Tyrael in more detail later. For now, I feel compelled to state that my personal commentary on Tyrael reflects my own view, and I would ask the readers to draw their own conclusions about him.

AURIEL, ARCHANGEL OF HOPE

Auriel is the most beloved of all angels. It is she who leads the sweet chorus of the High Heavens. She is said to be at the center of this chorus and to be the most lighthearted member of the Angiris Council. Auriel believes in the potential for good in all things, including the hearts of all sentient beings.

Auriel is not a pacifist. She does not shy away from strife, for she recognizes that conflict is the nature of this broken universe. There are many tales of her incredible feats in battle, breaching the walls of the Pandemonium Fortress alongside her fellow archangels to wrest the stronghold from Hell's grasp.

However, what makes Auriel unique is her ability to see harmony even in the midst of discord. She believes that victory for one side does not always mean defeat for the other. To her way of thinking, beyond each conflict lies the promise of healing, just as even in the dark of night one knows that the coming dawn will bring a new day.

I have read of heated arguments between Imperius and Tyrael that were put to rest only by Auriel's intervention. She did so not by scolding them or objecting to the use of violence, but by showing her comrades that resolution can open doors to new possibilities. For this archangel to temper the likes of Imperius and Tyrael, she must truly possess extraordinary patience and benevolence.

I have heard tales that during arguments and debates, Auriel will sometimes drape Al'maiesh, the Cord of Hope, around her comrades' shoulders to grant them clarity of thought and emotion. The cord is said to be a manifestation of Auriel's positive qualities. Pulsing with glowing runes from end to end, the long, serpentine ribbon can heal and energize those it touches. In battle, Auriel can just as quickly whip the cord through the ranks of her enemies, burning them with righteous fire.

Auriel, it seems, spends much of her time in the Gardens of Hope, a tranquil quarter of the High Heavens where angels go to clear their minds and find serenity. The trees in this area do not have leaves per se, but their canopies dance with shimmers of light and sound. At all times, an uplifting choir rings throughout the gardens. Those who hear it find their spirits in harmonious alignment with every other angel who dwells in the Heavens.

ITHERAEL, ARCHANGEL OF FATE

Archangels believe in fate, or destiny—the sense that all things are "written," and therefore knowable. Itherael has a unique ability to read the esoteric and arcane writings of fate. None of the others dare even try. To them, the visions are indecipherable.

By all available accounts, Itherael's prophecies are not always dark, and he holds a balanced view of all things.

Though his loyalty to the Angiris Council is unquestioned, Itherael has been described as inscrutable or aloof. It is suggested in the texts that Imperius has often sought to learn from Itherael the outcome of the Eternal Conflict. Itherael has maintained at all times a steadfast dedication to victory, but the writings tell us that he has never shared with Imperius his views on the ultimate fate of the never-ending war between the Heavens and the Hells.

It has also been observed that of all the archangels, Itherael is closest to Auriel.

It is written that the archangel of Fate is capable of predicting the actions of armies and even single opponents before those actions take place. More incredibly, Itherael can slow time itself. Whether this claim is to be taken literally or not, I do not know.

To further understand Itherael, it is necessary to speak of Talus'ar, the Scroll of Fate. It is this mystical object which Itherael consults in times of great need. Although it is a single scroll, accounts suggest that the information scrawled on the enchanted parchment changes based on the answers Itherael seeks.

Allegedly, this is made possible by a vast number of crystals Itherael possesses within the Library of Fate. These gems are reputed to be shards of the Crystal Arch, which is in turn believed by some scholars to be the spine of Anu.

Within the library, angel ascetics peer into the crystals, recording the visions they behold for Itherael to interpret.

Some records suggest that when Anu was blasted apart, its state of all-knowing was fragmented as well. If true, then it is possible for the crystals within the Library of Fate to provide visions of multiple possible futures.

Perhaps it is for this reason that Itherael is viewed as aloof or even indecisive, and that his predictions may sometimes seem flawed.

Also worth noting here is that since the discovery of Sanctuary, it is reported that Itherael has been unable to see the fate of the nephalem within his scroll, because they are not of the natural order of creation.

MALTHAEL,
ARCHANGEL OF WISDOM

Malthael is the most mysterious member of the Angiris Council. He is an intelligent and noble being who was once said to cherish all life, but the archangel is later described as melancholy, evasive, and at times even frightening.

Perhaps this is because he is bound to the truth of all things. His wisdom comes from seeing the myriad emotions and experiences that connect the universe. I believe Malthael's demeanor can be better understood through the following tract written by the mortal sage Furisaj, who sought out wisdom for the entirety of his life:

*In all things, there are two sides: motion and stillness,
emptiness and fullness, light and dark.*

*Alone each side is incomplete, but together they form the
totality of existence. Only through embracing the oneness
of all things can true wisdom be obtained.*

Malthael can at times be ponderous and slow to action, but he is revered by other angels for
his insight. He rarely speaks (and has thus become known as the silent angel), but when
he does, all those nearby stop to listen. His voice thrums with the harmony of the Heavens,
and those who hear it cannot help but become enraptured by its melody and the wisdom it
conveys. There are other reports I have uncovered which suggest that Malthael's demeanor
has darkened over time, and that his voice has become chilling and can provoke thoughts of
foreboding and feelings of angst. Again, we see the contrast associated with Malthael.

Due to the archangel's contemplative nature, it appears that he is slow to anger, but that has not
restricted him from playing a crucial role in the Eternal Conflict. In fact, Malthael is a peerless
combatant, so in tune with the nature of all things that he can deflect enemy attacks with only
the slightest use of force.

He is said to derive his insight from Chalad'ar, the Chalice of Wisdom. This vessel is not
like a cup of water that you or I would be familiar with. Rather, the chalice contains living
light that can never be depleted. By peering into its depths, Malthael can see the web of
connectivity that binds all things as one.

I have heard tales of Malthael staring into the chalice for years on end in his quarter of the
High Heavens, the Pools of Wisdom. The pools are infinitely deep wells of emotion. Those
who gaze into them see not their own reflection, but the sum total of emotion that all sentient
beings in the universe are experiencing at that moment. It is from these pools, I believe, that
Malthael draws to fill his chalice.

One intriguing fact concerning Malthael is that the darkening of his mood is said to have taken
place in the years following Sanctuary's creation. Did the birth of the nephalem somehow cloud
the archangel's eyes from wisdom, or did it open them to some new foreboding truth? Perhaps
Malthael's change in demeanor is connected to his chalice and the visions he beheld there? Or,
perhaps there is a connection between the nephalem and the chalice of which we are unaware.

Unfortunately, we may never know. I have read troubling accounts that Malthael disappeared
after the Worldstone's destruction (an event I will describe later in this tome). As I write this,
I cannot help but be reminded of the prophecy that "Wisdom shall be lost." I find it hard not to
view Malthael's sudden departure as yet another sign of the End of Days.

Monuments of Wonder

The illustrations I have provided here were pieced together from descriptions given by mystics who specialized in peering beyond the veil of our realm, for no mortal has yet set foot in the High Heavens.

Clearly, the artwork depicts a romanticized view of the Heavens, embraced by painters of the time. They portrayed comforting, majestic images of cloud and light. They created in meticulous detail infinite spaces of joy and possibility, a glorious realm that seems to enjoy a state of perpetual dawn.

I have combined some of these works with cryptic pieces of art acquired in the Mosaic period in order to inform our speculation and provide a more balanced view of the High Heavens and their major landmarks.

THE SILVER CITY

If the artwork of the great masters is to be believed, the Silver City is like a small world unto itself, a sprawling complex of glittering, soaring spires and sweeping buttresses. The magnificent architecture within it pulses with streams of light, and the entirety of it exists against a backdrop of radiant luminescence that stretches to infinity.

The contrasts between the High Heavens and the Burning Hells are obvious and striking, but there is one difference in particular that I wish to draw attention to: Unlike the Hells, which are broken into several realms whose borders shift and collide, the regions of the High Heavens are all centered within this one location, and their boundaries remain static.

To my knowledge, each member of the Angiris Council presides over a location within the Heavens, but it seems that the archangels and their domains exist in relative harmony. It is said that the Silver City is forever, that it will never change. It is eternal, the gleaming heart of the High Heavens, and it is an uplifting, living testament to the archangels' majesty.

THE CRYSTAL ARCH

High atop the Silver Spire, the tallest tower in the Heavens, sits the Crystal Arch, a wondrous structure that, as I discussed earlier, is believed to be the spine of the legendary Anu. Mystics have described the Arch as being composed of uncountable diamond facets that shimmer with a brilliance indescribable in mortal words.

If the ancient accounts are true, the Arch hums with a remnant of Anu's essence in a sublime chorus that permeates every corner of the High Heavens. Luminous bands flare off the Arch in perfect synchronization with its music, occasionally manifesting as new angels.

Unlike demons, who constantly war with each other, angels seek harmony among their own kind. If they are truly born from the Crystal Arch, then perhaps that would explain their penchant for order and balance.

The Arch is said to birth angels only during moments of perfect harmony in the Heavens. How often this happens, and what exactly causes this perfect harmony, are questions I cannot answer. There have been many periods of disharmony in the High Heavens, but I do not know whether this state has prohibited new angels from being created.

In other words, it is unclear whether these descriptions of the Arch are to be taken literally. The information I have found provides an interesting vision of the High Heavens, but one must always be careful of the balance between mythology and metaphor.

I can tell you that from the mystics of Aranoch to the priests of the Skovos Isles, all agree that an echo of the Heavens can be heard at the height of meditation. I find myself wondering if this echo might be the divine harmony that emanates directly from the Crystal Arch.

THE DIAMOND GATES

As with the Crystal Arch, the Diamond Gates are said to be composed of glittering, crystalline facets.

We are told by ancient sources that the ravening multitudes of the Burning Hells have fought their way to the Diamond Gates on more than one occasion. There is no existing account, however, of the Diamond Gates having ever been breached.

If the writings are true, then no enemy has ever set foot past the gates and into the Silver City. The greatest and most elite warriors of the Heavenly Host maintain a tireless vigil at the gates, standing ready to repel any who would despoil the radiance of the High Heavens.

The Silver City, the Crystal Arch, the Diamond Gates. I can scarcely imagine what it must be like to behold these magnificent structures in person, or how it might feel to cross bridges of light, or bask in the glory of cascading fountains of music and harmony.

After all, how could I, a mere mortal, ever hope to comprehend such splendor?

Sanctuary, the Mortal Realm

Inarius and the Worldstone

As I study the end times, seeking ways to forestall what I have come to feel is inevitable, I believe it is more important than ever to understand the origins of our world.

In the later sections of the *Books of Kalan* is an epic poem that tells of the renegade angel Inarius. The accounts of Inarius' life state that he was an advisor to the Angiris Council, serving under the command of Tyrael, archangel of Justice. It is further written that after eons of battle and witnessing countless acts of brutality, Inarius came to the conclusion that the Eternal Conflict was unjust and that his part in it must come to an end. He quickly resolved to seek out others who might share his view. In time he recruited not only angels but, incredibly, demons as well, and convinced them to join his blasphemous venture.

There was one among them, however, who stood out above all others. While wounded or marooned on some broken outpost of the Pandemonium Fortress, Inarius arranged to meet the demoness Lilith. Lilith, who had suffered the hatred of her father, Mephisto, from time immemorial, had long awaited an opportunity to rebel.

And so it was that something extraordinary and unprecedented happened: For the first time ever, combatants in the Eternal Conflict not only set aside their differences but also formed a union. Drawn together despite opposing forces, they had discovered common ground.

It is difficult for my mind to fully grasp, but the legends tell us that Inarius and Lilith fell in love. Incredibly, that single alliance would alter the course of the war, of reality itself—indeed, of all existence.

Inarius and Lilith both pledged themselves to the other and vowed to escape the Eternal Conflict. United in purpose, they gathered their fellow renegades and either led a campaign to capture the Worldstone or used some misdirection to gain entrance to its guarded chamber within the Pandemonium Fortress.

What happened next I will attempt to convey as best I can through the hazy curtains of both time and myth.

The Creation of Sanctuary

The *Books of Kalan* state the following:

> Inarius and his new companions altered the frequency or dimensional alignment of the Worldstone, using its power to conceal it from the angels and demons still fighting the Eternal Conflict. They shifted the massive crystal into a pocket dimension, and there they shaped a garden paradise around it: a world of refuge they would call Sanctuary.

We cannot say how this feat was accomplished, as the means of Inarius' actions remain unknown. But it is known from the *Books of Kalan* and other, lesser sources from this time that the Eternal Conflict briefly came to a grinding halt over the Worldstone's disappearance.

For my own part, it is amusing to think of what it must have been like for the forces of Heaven and Hell to fight their way to the Worldstone's usual location, only to find it missing. I would speculate that for a time both groups must have accused the other of stealing it, until they were finally convinced that their opponents were just as confused as they.

The account given, supported by events which would come eons later, is that Inarius shaped Mount Arreat as a kind of protective shell around the Worldstone—and from there the rest of the world as we know it was formed.

There the Worldstone remained until recent times, when the archangel Tyrael destroyed the sacred crystal and much of Mount Arreat surrounding it. But I get ahead of myself. This matter will be addressed in a later section, for the implications of the Worldstone's destruction and its ripple effects are felt by us to this very day.

As noted earlier, I once beheld the Pandemonium Fortress with my own eyes. I have done my best to illustrate the fortress here, however warped and distorted my memories of it might be.

61

Rise of the Nephalem

That which happened next is of the utmost importance to us mortals. Indeed, had it not happened, we would not exist, for something previously unimagined took place: Inarius and Lilith mated and created offspring. And though they were the first, in time other renegade angels and demons were drawn together as well.

And, alas, we are of our fathers and mothers, alike and yet opposite, one decay and the other light. Indeed, the union of the angel and demon created a third essence. And we are those children. We are the nephalem. We exist as half angel and half demon, yet fully a new entity. And because of our lineage, they loved us. And because of our difference, they feared us. Within the trembling balance between love and fear is the relation of us to our fathers and mothers.

I gain much of what follows from fragments of the ancient tome of the druids, the *Scéal Fada*.

The first generations of nephalem were called the ancients. It is believed that they set out exploring, seeking answers, attempting to understand their curious world, and that they adopted numerous philosophies as they spread across Sanctuary.

One of these ancients was Bul-Kathos. Renowned for his immense strength, enormous size, bravery, and fortitude, Bul-Kathos is revered to this very day by the barbarians who settled at Mount Arreat. Indeed, the present-day barbarians epitomize many of the ancient's traits: great size, strength, tenacity, and an iron will.

Barbarian myths tell of Bul-Kathos' younger brother (elsewhere referred to as a trusted confidant) named Vasily. One myth in particular paints Vasily as a frustrated sibling who struck out into the wild and developed an affinity for nature. In this version of the tale, Vasily's descendants became the druids.

We know of other nephalem of this age also. Esu, a woman drawn to the power and ferocity of the elements, gained mastery over the powers of storm, earth, fire, and water through intense meditation. Ages later, her followers would rise as the feared sorceresses of Kehjistan.

Finally, we come to Rathma, a brooding, solitary
being who sought out the deep recesses of the world.
He studied the cycle of life and death and taught it to
those willing to venture into his subterranean habitat.
Rathma is the patron of the necromancers, and he values the
Balance of light and dark above all things.

I feel compelled to state for the sake of clarity that thousands,
or perhaps tens of thousands, of ancients doubtlessly existed during
this time. It is possible or even likely that they possessed abilities
beyond our understanding.

Who's to say what tales of these demigods have been lost over time?

The powers of the ancients had an unexpected effect on their
otherworldly parents. The renegade angels and demons began to see
that their nephalem children were far more powerful than they. This, for
obvious reasons, raised concern amongst them that the nephalem might
not only become a threat but also draw the attention of the Heavens and
Hells from which they hid.

We must remember that by commingling, these angels and demons had
spawned what their masters would deem the ultimate blasphemy, and the
defectors were convinced that they would be destroyed if their hidden
refuge was ever discovered.

Because of this, conflict arose, as many of the renegades held the opinion
that their nephalem offspring should be destroyed, while others believed
their children should be spared. This dissension troubled Inarius, who
called for a period of reflection. And so his followers agreed to consider
the matter in solitude.

*Rathma: The necromancers who venerate this
nephalem have depicted him in the form of a great
writhing serpent. Is this mere legend, or did he
somehow take on this strange inhuman visage?*

The Purge

Though the following tale strains credibility, I will transcribe it anyway:

*Lilith, the first mother of the nephalem, was driven into a mad
frenzy by the threat of her children's extinction. She morphed into
a far more horrific form than any had ever seen—of tooth and
claw, of spike and blade—and hunted down her fellow renegades.
She ruthlessly murdered each and every follower of Inarius, leaving
only him to discover the carnage she had wrought.*

*Inarius was horrified by the loss of his comrades and the terrible
deed that his lover had committed. Though enraged, he could not
bring himself to kill Lilith, but instead banished her from the
sanctuary they had made.*

*Inarius then attuned the Worldstone to cause the powers of the
nephalem to diminish over time. He then disappeared—though
some say that he still walks amongst us in a form more closely
resembling our own.*

—Anonymous text found uncatalogued
in the Great Library at Caldeum

As I have said before, untangling myth from history is a tricky business.
According to the arcana that have found their way into my possession, the
powers of the nephalem did, indeed, fade over the course of generations.
Today, our mortal bloodlines are the result of this great diminishment.

Given the propensity for both good and evil in humankind, it is clear to me
that some measure of our ancestors still resonates within us. And yet
I wonder, is it possible for humanity to evolve into something wholly
extraordinary, or are we bound to the fate of our forefathers?

I will speak more of Inarius and Lilith later, for both would return to play
vital roles in the history of the world they created.

Take heed of this, Leah, for while we might be only distant descendants of the original nephalem, I believe that mankind has the potential to unlock these awesome powers once again.

Ancient History
The Birth of Civilization

Years became decades, and then centuries, leading to millennia of time elapsed. Generations of nephalem, even with the remarkable long lives they were said to have possessed, passed away. With each generation, those events which might have been truth turned to legend, eventually settling into myth. The angels and demons faded from consciousness. The nephalem themselves slowly became mere mortals not unlike ourselves.

Humankind began to populate the world. As with its nephalem ancestors, humanity set about building cities of its own and collecting knowledge from the far corners of Sanctuary.

Various texts recount that the druidic followers of Vasily retreated into the northern forests of Scosglen, where they formed centers of learning to achieve harmony with the natural world. Elsewhere, priests from the cult of Rathma observed their esoteric rites within a vast subterranean city beneath the eastern jungles. Powerful covens of Esu witches strove to attune themselves to the world's elemental forces in their pursuit of what they deemed "perfect" magic.

Numerous exotic religious systems also flourished during this period. The mystic Taan mage clan and the superstitious Skatsimi cult practiced their beliefs in hidden temples throughout the east. All across Sanctuary, evolving cultures and civilizations formed and embraced their own explanations for the universe and its mysteries, giving rise to two divergent views—mysticism and faith.

In its simplest terms, mysticism is man's study of science and magic, the seen and unseen forces which shape the world around us. Even more than that, the root of mysticism is man's desire to become the master of his own destiny. Counter to this is faith, the view that man must put his trust in powers beyond mortal understanding to determine his fate and establish ethical and moral guidelines to live by.

Dear reader, the clash between these ideologies is at the core of humankind's existence. It has shaped our history in profound and irrevocable ways, and I believe it will continue to do so for as long as humans walk this world.

As proof, we need only look to the beginning of recorded history, which was ignited by a surge in mysticism. Magic in all its forms was studied and formalized into distinct schools and disciplines. In Kehjan (what is now Kehjistan), these schools evolved into mage clans, the most prominent of which were the Vizjerei, the Ennead, and the Ammuit.

The Vizjerei are discussed in detail later in this tome. The Ennead was a school that focused on enchantments and transmutation of matter. Its members used practical application to affect the world around them, while the Ammuit clan dabbled in illusion and strove to manipulate reality and our perception of it.

It is important to note that not all members of the mage clans were sorcerers. The clans were ethnically and culturally distinct societies with their own laws, customs, artisans, and merchants. Beyond that, each clan was defined by its adherence to a particular school of magic. While only the mage caste studied this vocation, each clan's discipline nonetheless pervaded all corners of society, evidencing itself in things such as art and regional vernacular.

The burgeoning power of the mage clans made their involvement in Kehjan's ruling affairs inevitable. The Al'Raqish, or Mage Council, an organization boasting members from each of the major clans, was formed to rule alongside the kingdom's monarchy and its powerful guilds. The council's leadership rotated to a different clan representative every new moon.

Despite the violent feuds and deep-seated prejudice that appears to have existed among the clans, the council thrived for generations. I have read accounts that eventually the head members of the kingdom's royal line became little more than puppet rulers. True power resided with the mage clans.

Sadly, this era of relative peace and stability was not to last. Man's desire to plumb the secrets of the world and the unseen realms beyond it would soon lead to calamity.

Sanctuary Revealed

The Vizjerei were convinced that spirits dwelled on Sanctuary and in places outside the physical world. While the clan's sorcerers could not directly commune with these entities, they believed contact was possible. Thus, the driving goal of the Vizjerei became to perfect the arts of conjuring and summoning spirits.

For years, the clan conducted experiments and carried out empirical research into the practices of druids and necromancers—both of which successfully contacted spirits in their own way. Yet for all of the combined intellect and dedication of the Vizjerei mages, they could hear only a whisper of the beings they sought.

Everything changed with one unassuming Vizjerei sorcerer named Jere Harash. I take the following account of Harash's life from the personal journals of Dumal Lunnash, who wrote extensively on the earlier periods of the Vizjerei:

> Jere Harash was a most forgettable member of the Vizjerei sorcerers. As a young acolyte, he aspired to one day represent his clan on the Mage Council, but he was always outshined by his more talented peers. His growing frustrations came to a head when his parents and sister were killed during a short-lived feud between the Vizjerei and Ammuit clans.
>
> As his heart roiled with anger and rage at the tragedy, Harash reached out to the spirits and made contact, succeeding where so many of his fellow sorcerers had failed. Yet the entity he summoned into our world was one neither he nor the other Vizjerei could have ever fathomed—a demon of pure hate and malice. And with that, the once-ineffectual Jere Harash was etched into the annals of history forever.

I find it interesting that this excerpt does not match the public records (some even written by Lunnash himself) of Harash. These describe Harash as having been a young boy who gleaned insight into summoning from a dream. Even the being he contacted was referred to as a "spirit of the dead."

Whether the Vizjerei originally knew that the summoned being was a demon is unclear, but I have no doubt they believed it was something more than an ancestor's spirit. From my research, I have found that the Vizjerei worked feverishly to mask the truth of what had been discovered, even going so far as to write false histories of Harash and some of their early interactions with the "dead."

I can only surmise that Harash's success, in reality, hinged on the dark emotions he was feeling at the time. Perhaps his anger and rage somehow attuned him to one of the Burning Hells' realms. Whatever the root cause, Harash quickly recognized the perils of the murderous creature he had summoned. After restraining it with binding spells, he informed the Vizjerei elders of his discovery.

It is of utmost importance to note that at the moment of Harash's breakthrough, the Prime Evils of the Burning Hells became aware of Sanctuary's existence for the first time.

This was, of course, unknown to the Vizjerei. Even after the demon had been summoned, there was much controversy among them concerning the new art Harash had discovered. Some of the sorcerers feared that these dangerous entities could not be fully controlled and posed a threat to the entire world.

The one thing the clan members all agreed upon was that the existence of demons should be kept secret. This explains their retelling of Harash's discovery and their willingness to adopt the lie that they were merely communing with spirits of the dead. By doing so, the clan could claim innocence of any wrongdoing should the powers it was experimenting with lead to disaster. So successful were they in this farce that the Vizjerei eventually became known as the Spirit Clan.

The Vizjerei eventually grew confident that if they could control one demon, they could control others. The clan's sorcerers set about summoning more and more of the Burning Hells' minions into Sanctuary for short periods. While the clan had no intentions of using the demons as weapons, the mages concluded that there was much to be learned from these creatures about the universe and new forms of magic.

Alas, as we have witnessed so many times throughout history, humankind's insatiable greed and lust for power took hold of the Vizjerei. Once having tasted of forbidden demonic powers, the clan decided that with its newfound abilities, it could enslave Hell's denizens and use them to dominate not only Kehjan, but the entire world as well.

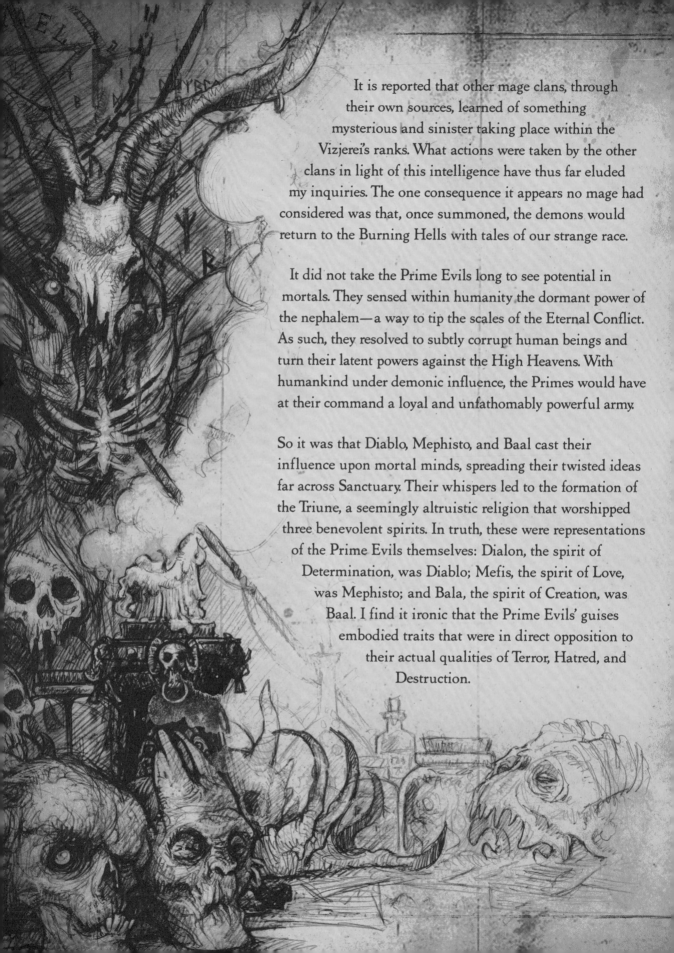

It is reported that other mage clans, through their own sources, learned of something mysterious and sinister taking place within the Vizjereï's ranks. What actions were taken by the other clans in light of this intelligence have thus far eluded my inquiries. The one consequence it appears no mage had considered was that, once summoned, the demons would return to the Burning Hells with tales of our strange race.

It did not take the Prime Evils long to see potential in mortals. They sensed within humanity the dormant power of the nephalem—a way to tip the scales of the Eternal Conflict. As such, they resolved to subtly corrupt human beings and turn their latent powers against the High Heavens. With humankind under demonic influence, the Primes would have at their command a loyal and unfathomably powerful army.

So it was that Diablo, Mephisto, and Baal cast their influence upon mortal minds, spreading their twisted ideas far across Sanctuary. Their whispers led to the formation of the Triune, a seemingly altruistic religion that worshipped three benevolent spirits. In truth, these were representations of the Prime Evils themselves: Dialon, the spirit of Determination, was Diablo; Mefis, the spirit of Love, was Mephisto; and Bala, the spirit of Creation, was Baal. I find it ironic that the Prime Evils' guises embodied traits that were in direct opposition to their actual qualities of Terror, Hatred, and Destruction.

The popularity of the religion grew rapidly, and before long a large percentage of ancient Kehjan's populace had flocked to the Triune. The rank-and-file members of the church, of course, did not realize that their patron spirits were Lords of the Burning Hells. Key to the Primes' deception was that the Triune falsely stood for the principles of unity and humankind's innate power.

The religion constructed a magnificent Grand Temple in Kehjan. The sprawling triangular edifice boasted three high towers, each of which was dedicated to one of the Triune's spirits. The organization was so devoted to giving the impression of being a peaceful group that it even referred to the temple's warriors as Peace Warders.

Only the highest-ranking members of the Triune knew the truth: Behind the facade of Determination, Love, and Creation was a vile cult which practiced all manner of demonic rituals. It was known to lure in unsuspecting initiates and practice fiendish acts of torture on them for the perverse thrill of its true Prime Evil masters. With these horrors in mind, it should come as no surprise that the religion was led by none other than Lucion, the son of Mephisto I mentioned earlier in this tome.

The Triune's rapid growth perplexed the mage clans and other institutions that had, until then, held an uncontested sway over Kehjan's populace. From accounts I have read of this era, it seems that these groups believed the Triune to be nothing more than a passing fancy. Therefore, they simply stood by as more and more victims were lured into the jaws of the Prime Evils' false religion.

As a final note, one might ask whether Diablo, Mephisto, and Baal knew the truth concerning humanity's divine parentage. From what I have gleaned from my studies, it is unclear. I have discovered, however, that the Prime Evils made a point of keeping Sanctuary's existence a secret from as many of their lesser brethren as they could. This lack of trust would sour the relations among the Lords of the Burning Hells, and, I believe, lead in some part to the Dark Exile, an event which I will write on later.

The Sin War

It is written that the angel Inarius, the first father of humankind, wandered the world in grief for ages after the massacre of his fellow renegade angels and demons by his lover, Lilith. (This event, the Purge, is described earlier in this tome.)

Inarius had observed humanity, watching us face challenges and overcome obstacles. It is heavily suggested by some accounts that he had even come to favor mortals, for he saw us, unlike our ancient ancestors, as no threat.

It is further stated that when Inarius learned of the Triune religion, he recognized the Prime Evils' deception immediately, and feared not only for his own safety but also for that of his adopted children should Heaven become aware of humanity's existence.

And so the texts tell us that Inarius created his own religion to counter the influence of the Triune. Taking on the mantle of the Prophet, Inarius founded a gospel based on the tenets of tolerance, cooperation, and unity. He disseminated this doctrine from his Cathedral of Light, gaining fame for his youthful physical perfection and spreading the church's influence through angelic powers of persuasion. Soon, between them, the Triune and the Cathedral of Light held sway over much of the eastern lands.

Having studied the matter in great detail, I conclude that Inarius' founding of the Cathedral of Light is the true beginning of the Sin War.

Much of what I will relate of the Sin War and its history is taken from the mysterious *Books of Kalan*. The identity of their author, except his name, is unknown, as is the exact time of authorship. It is my belief that the books were written during the time of the Sin War and later edited and compiled by other unknown hands.

The Sin War, at its inception, was not waged on physical battlefields. It was a struggle between the Triune and the Cathedral of Light to claim the hearts and souls of humankind.

Agents of both religions carried their messages to the people, building bases of power, constructing monuments, and winning the absolute loyalty of faithful supplicants.

Into the midst of this battle for dominance came a single human, Uldyssian, a man who would break the cycle and rise to not only challenge both religions but also ultimately bring an end to the Sin War through a staggering chain of events, shaking the foundations of both the Heavens and the Hells in the process.

Uldyssian's story began in a small village where he lived with his youngest brother, Mendeln, and a few close friends. It was here that Uldyssian first discovered his nephalem powers, while defending a woman named Lylia from a priest representing the Cathedral of Light.

Uldyssian learned that he was capable of awakening nephalem powers in others. He traveled from town to town, demonstrating to others that they did not need either the Triune or the Prophet and his Cathedral of Light. And as Uldyssian's abilities evolved, so too did the powers of his family, friends, and followers, who would come to be known as the edyrem, or "those who have seen."

While pursued by both the Triune and the Cathedral of Light, Uldyssian cultivated his powers, growing in strength day by day, until his abilities were far beyond those of any other human.

Lylia, however, was soon revealed to be none other than Lilith, the demon daughter of Mephisto, returned from exile. It was Lilith who had awakened the nephalem abilities in Uldyssian; it was her desire to empower mortals so they might drive both Inarius and the agents of the Burning Hells from Sanctuary, but she was willing to sacrifice mortal lives to see this plan unfold. Once her true nature was revealed, Lilith departed, though she would return over the course of the war to torment Uldyssian again.

At this time, the forces of the Triune clashed repeatedly with Uldyssian and his edyrem, and it was soon revealed that the Triune was held under the sway of demonic influence. Uldyssian declared war on the Triune, obliterating its churches and decimating its holy armies.

Observe, dear reader, that the mortal Uldyssian succeeded in bringing the Sin War to a halt. Humankind, not angels or demons, would ultimately win the Sin War.

Uldyssian soon learned of the Worldstone, and achieved the unthinkable, altering its attunement to allow the powers of his edyrem to flourish. The edyrem then came into conflict with Inarius himself. The battle between mortals and Inarius' forces rocked the core of our world.

It is said that Inarius, in danger of losing his battle with Uldyssian, panicked, realizing how wrong he had been about humanity's weakness. In that moment, he feared that mortals were even more dangerous and abominable than the ancients.

It was then that Tyrael himself intervened. Reacting to the seeming injustice of Uldyssian's actions against Inarius, Tyrael called forth the angelic Host of the High Heavens. Hundreds of angels descended upon Sanctuary. Much to the surprise of everyone present, however, the ground erupted as the Burning Hells joined the battle as well. The fears of Lilith and Inarius were realized as the Eternal Conflict raged on the world of man.

Uldyssian unleashed the whole of his power, releasing a seemingly impossible amount of energy, driving the forces of both Heaven and Hell back to their domains, and demonstrating once and for all that humankind truly had the ability to alter the very fabric of our universe.

Uldyssian realized that the power he and his edyrem possessed was tearing Sanctuary apart. It was too much, gained too quickly. He felt also that he was losing himself— that his nephalem birthright was consuming his humanity—and he saw in that moment the potential for nephalem power to do the same to all of humankind.

And so, in an act of the purest selflessness and sacrifice, which proved beyond a doubt that some humanity still remained within him, Uldyssian brought the raging energies back into himself, then released them one final time. The release of those energies negated his very being.

It has been suggested in the *Books of Kalan* that Uldyssian's final release of energy flooded the Worldstone, resetting it, and thereby stripping his followers of their nephalem powers. And so it was that Uldyssian had chosen the human heart over godhood and ultimately gave his life so that humanity might survive.

In the wake of these incredible events, I can only imagine that the Burning Hells were emboldened to discover that their suspicions of humankind's potential were proved correct.

As for the angels, it is said that the Angiris Council voted on whether humanity should be allowed to live. It is reported that Imperius voted to exterminate our race. Malthael abstained, and so his vote was not counted, while Auriel and Itherael voted on our behalf. Imperius was confident that Tyrael would vote to eliminate humanity, and he knew that even if the deliberation ended in a tie, humankind would be eradicated.

And so it fell to the archangel Tyrael to cast the deciding vote. I believe that it was here that Tyrael broke from his rigid outlook. He had witnessed Uldyssian's heroic and very human act, and he became fascinated with mortal hearts, believing that perhaps the universe cannot be defined by laws alone. Tyrael saw in us the possibility for complete ruin—but hope as well, for us to become what many of the angels themselves wished they could be.

And so it was that the archangel of Justice cast his vote in favor of sparing humankind.

As humanity's right to exist was assured, a truce was brokered between the Angiris Council and the Lords of the Burning Hells. As a condition of this truce, Inarius was delivered to the demons for mutilation and eternal torment.

As for the edyrem, it is written that the angels removed all memories of these events from their minds. Their nephalem powers were forgotten, and mortal life returned to some semblance of normality.

And what of Lilith? Accounts suggest that earlier in the conflict, before the Prophet (or the Veiled Prophet, as a few scholars would later call him) clashed with Uldyssian, Inarius had banished Lilith once again. There are no further accounts of her interfering in the affairs of mortals.

Though the Sin War faded quietly into history, it is imperative that we recognize its import, for it stands as a testament to the sheer power that all human beings carry within them. And, I would argue, it is a war that echoes within each of us to this very day.

The Mage Clan Wars

In the decades following the Sin War, Kehjan sought to distance itself from the events of that near-apocalyptic conflict. To this end, the people renamed their land Kehjistan.

As the kingdom started anew, mage clans reasserted the control they had previously held over the east. The greatest lessons learned by the Ennead and Ammuit clans from the time of the Triune and the Cathedral of Light were simple: No mage clan must ever again summon demons into the world, and if humanity had anything to say about it, the Heavens and Hells must stay out of mortal affairs forever.

Legends hold that before the Sin War there had been seven major and seven minor mage clans, but following Uldyssian's sacrifice only three maintained a strong influence—the same three that had been the most prominent years before: the Vizjerei, the Ennead, and the Ammuit. It was the Vizjerei clan, however, that once again rose to greatest success and soon counted thousands of active sorcerers among its ranks.

It is incredible to look back upon this era and consider the prosperity of the Vizjerei. After all, what were the roots of the Vizjerei's success? Conjuring and summoning. One might even say that much of the peace and grandeur of this golden age was built on the enslavement of demons generations before.

It is no surprise, then, that the Vizjerei operated under close scrutiny, as the other mage clans made clear to the original conjuring school that if it grew arrogant and tempted fate once again, there would be dire ramifications.

The reality of the nephalem and the involvement of the Heavens and Hells in the Sin War were kept from the general populace. It was publicly stated (and reinforced by those edyrem whose memories had been erased) that a plague had claimed the lives of those lost in the Sin War. Nevertheless, the truth was known by some, and it was generally recognized by these people that blind faith and religiosity during the war had not averted the disaster. In fact, it was not long before the prevailing opinion was that humankind's embracing of religion had set the events of the war in motion.

There was no more room for faith. The citizens would believe now only what they could behold with their own eyes. Popular religions were suppressed as the people embraced the mage clans, who relied on the empirical and the quantifiable. The kingdom took comfort in a system that valued reason and practical research above all, and so it was that once again the Al'Raqish, the Mage Council, enjoyed great success and power, governing the land in cooperation with the royal line from the eastern capital of Viz-jun.

Remaining artworks tell us that this was a time of inspiration, investigation, and, as the shadow of fear slowly passed, enlightenment. Oh, to have lived in such a time! We can only imagine how wonderful this era must have been. Mages in magnificent robes walked the streets, and all turned to look upon them. Great buildings were erected, and civilization flourished.

It was then, in this time of unprecedented peace and prosperity, that the Vizjerei would once again imperil humankind. The earliest clue of this is evidenced in the following, an unsigned letter found within the ruins of an Ammuit academy near Caldeum, presumably sent from an Ennead official:

I share this matter in the strictest confidence.

The following account has been verified by our most trustworthy source: It was only two nights ago that five high-ranking Vizjerei conjurers were overheard in the deepest recesses of the Yshari Sanctum, chanting incantations and conducting what could only have been a ritual of summoning. A small tremor was felt soon after, followed by the sound of throat-rending screams. Where five conjurers had entered, only three emerged hours later.

It goes without saying that these activities are unacceptable. The Vizjerei have disregarded multiple warnings and are clearly revisiting past sins, setting them on a course that will result in the destruction of all that we have labored to build. Measures are being taken on our side. The Vizjerei will soon lie in a bed of their own making. I have been led to believe that in a circumstance such as this we might count on your support.

I truly hope such claims are valid, brother constable, for now is the time to end the Vizjerei's recklessness once and for all.

Evidence suggests that soon after this letter was written, assassins were sent out against key members of the Vizjerei by both the Ennead and the Ammuit, and that several officials from those clans were brutally murdered in retaliation.

The conflict escalated further when an argument among clan representatives at a meeting of the Al'Raqish erupted into a battle that resulted in multiple deaths.

Soon, the blood of all three clans was being spilled on the streets. The violence surged, until the Ennead and Ammuit clans in Caldeum gathered their forces and stormed the Vizjerei main academy in Viz-jun. When the dust settled, not one wall of the academy was left standing, and not a single Vizjerei mage there was left alive. This incident was the spark that set off the Mage Clan Wars proper.

Battles flared across the eastern lands. The Vizjerei Ruling Council fled the capital, went into hiding, and focused on consolidating its forces. The coalition of Ennead and Ammuit forces won several victories against isolated pockets of Vizjerei combatants. The two clans then directed the entirety of their combined might against the Vizjerei's main force.

Hopelessly outnumbered, the Vizjerei were quickly trapped and seemed on the verge of annihilation. It was then that the true plan of the conjurers was revealed as they unleashed the one weapon no other clan had dared to wield: demons.

The balance of power quickly shifted as multitudes of Ennead and Ammuit troops were obliterated. Horrific nightmare-creatures from the deepest pits of the Burning Hells waded through the opposing clans, cutting a bloody swath. The Ennead and the Ammuit retreated as the Vizjerei pursued them all the way back to the capital of Viz-jun.

It is here that we must take a moment to focus on the story of two brothers, Horazon and Bartuc, for it was the actions of these siblings that would ultimately decide the outcome of the Mage Clan Wars. The following details were among very few passed on to me by my ancestor Jered Cain in the books of the Horadrim:

> Bartuc was a particularly ruthless mage who had earned the epithet "Warlord of Blood" for bathing in the blood of his slaughtered enemies. It is said that his armor was empowered with a demonic sentience. During the final battles of the Mage Clan Wars, Bartuc had become an unstoppable force, instilling fear not only in the opposing clans but in his own people as well.

> Horazon, who had delighted in breaking the wills of the demons he had summoned, realized that Bartuc's path would ultimately lead to ruin. Demonic corruption spread throughout the Vizjerei ranks. The hellspawn that Bartuc continued to summon lacked any

kind of control, destroying literally everything in their path, for Bartuc believed that the demons were humankind's masters, and that loyalty to them would be generously rewarded. Horazon reached the conclusion that even if the Vizjerei won the wars, there would soon be nothing of civilization left, and that the clan's only legacy would be death or enslavement to the Burning Hells.

And so it was that just when victory for the Vizjerei seemed assured, the Ruling Council resolved to relieve Bartuc of his command. Civil war erupted within the troubled mage clan as Bartuc turned his forces against his own people. After many hard-fought battles, Bartuc's contingent took the upper hand. The Warlord of Blood then set his armies to the task of conquering Viz-jun.

The final battle between Bartuc and the Vizjerei took place just outside the capital's towering gates. And just when it seemed that the entire clan would fail to defeat Bartuc, his brother Horazon answered the challenge.

The cataclysmic battle between the two siblings brought the walls of Viz-jun down around them. The city was leveled, and the death toll numbered in the hundreds of thousands.

But as the fire, smoke, and unholy bloody mist cleared, Bartuc, Warlord of Blood, lay dead with Horazon standing over his brother's gore-covered corpse.

Following the death of Bartuc, the grieving Horazon was keenly aware of the inherent tragedies of summoning. He realized that the corruption of hearts and civilizations would never end as long as the agents of the Burning Hells had access to our world.

My ancestor left an interesting postscript to the story of Horazon. He says, "Following the battle of Viz-jun, Horazon crafted for himself a hideaway which he called the Arcane Sanctuary, a retreat where the prying eyes of Hell could never find him. There he lived apart from the world, quietly studying the arcane and ultimately fading into the shrouded mists of legend."

THE AFTERMATH OF THE MAGE CLAN WARS

Whatever the true fate of Horazon, we have graphic accounts of the magnificent city of Viz-jun reduced to rubble, and with the destruction of the city also came the end of the mage clan system of government. Mages, who had been so revered by the people, were now exiled and in some extreme cases executed on sight. (In fact, in an unprecedented move, the surviving Vizjerei renounced summoning forever. To ensure that this new edict would stand, the clan deployed mage slayers, known as the Viz-Jaq'taar, to eliminate renegade Vizjerei wherever they might be found.) Many mages fled from the cities to eke out an existence in smaller towns or alone in the mountains and deserts. Certainly, some mage clans remained; even today, a few scattered Vizjerei still exist, but only in a pale and diminished form.

As with all traumas in history, each age breeds its opposite. The Age of Magic was replaced by the Age of Faith. Disgusted with the mages' reckless pursuit of power, the angry citizenry of Kehjistan looted the mage clans' holdings and tore down their bastions of power, with the exception of the Yshari Sanctum, in Caldeum. It alone survived the riotous purge, due to its more remote location. Overall, the vast arcane libraries and the innumerable tomes of occult knowledge throughout Kehjistan were destroyed, while laws were passed forbidding the use of magic. It is fair to say that the age of the mages had ended.

The Dark Exile

In truth, it is difficult to speak authoritatively about the event known as the Dark Exile, as it is alleged to have taken place in the Burning Hells, far from mortal eyes. In any case, the Dark Exile refers to a civil war that raged within the Burning Hells between the Prime and Lesser Evils.

It is said that the motivation for this conflict was the Lesser Evils' fury over the Primes having abandoned the Eternal Conflict in favor of weaponizing humankind's nephalem potential.

Believing that they were innately superior to mortal kind, and that their war against the High Heavens was theirs alone to fight, the Lesser Evils enacted a brilliant stratagem to overthrow the Primes. Led by Azmodan, the Lord of Sin, and Belial, the Lord of Lies, the rebel demons claimed dominion over much of the Burning Hells.

To their credit, the Prime Evils fought with devastating power, annihilating a third of Hell's treacherous legions. But in the end, weakened and bodiless, the Primes were banished to the mortal realm, where Azmodan hoped they would remain trapped forever.

Furthermore, Azmodan believed that with the Three set loose upon humanity, the angels would be forced to turn their focus upon the mortal plane, thus potentially leaving the gates of Heaven vulnerable to attack.

One account of the Dark Exile states that the Lesser Evils' hour of triumph did not last long. Relations between Azmodan and Belial quickly soured as they began arguing over who should ascend to the highest rank of the Burning Hells. When the bickering turned to violence, their pact was forgotten. The remaining denizens of the Hells found their support divided between the Lesser Evils, and before long another bloody civil war was under way.

Yet there are some who say that there was no falling-out between Azmodan and Belial, and that they are conspiring to subjugate all life to their will. While it is more comforting to believe that they turned on each other, I submit that it is best for us to believe that the two are still in league and at this moment are plotting an attack on the mortal realm.

As the answers to these disputes might lead to a clearer understanding of the end times, I will investigate further, but such inquiry will be difficult. We mortals have no direct access to knowledge of the machinations of the Burning Hells.

Also, as I am no expert on the inner workings of the High Heavens, either, I can only imagine what it must have been like for Tyrael to discover that the Prime Evils had been banished to the unsuspecting world of men.

By the time Tyrael learned the truth, the Primes had already been wreaking havoc on Sanctuary for decades. Subtly, they had been turning brother against brother and nation against nation, inciting wars and unrest amongst the lands of Kehjistan.

Knowing that the Sin War had resulted in the sparing of humankind by a margin of one vote, Tyrael did not dare inform the Angiris Council that the powers of Hell now threatened to corrupt humanity once again. He knew that, somehow, he had to intervene without alerting his angelic brethren and prevent the Prime Evils from influencing mortal men. On behalf of humankind, the archangel of Justice would become the maverick of Heaven.

The Hunt for the Three

Much of what follows concerning the Horadrim comes from writings passed down through my family from my ancestor Jered Cain in a collection of documents stored in an ancient chest. One day I should like to make these documents available, but I fear that they might contain information that even now, nearly three centuries later, may be dangerous should they fall into the wrong hands.

As to their accuracy, I can say that every fact in them is supported by what I have encountered in my travels in the form of contemporary texts, artifacts, and geography. And, to be quite honest, much of their content has been extremely relevant to my own experience as one of the few survivors of the horrors in Tristram (which I shall detail for you at a later time).

The Horadrim were a band of mages drawn from the remnants of the scattered mage clans and empowered by the archangel Tyrael to hunt down and contain the three Prime Evils. By the accounts of both my ancestor Jered and his colleague Nor Tiraj, the original Horadrim were strangers selected not due to any particular wisdom or reverence but because they were those most likely to succeed in carrying out Tyrael's mission.

The first group of Horadrim was small. Some say the number was seven; some say the number was twelve. Both numbers might be correct, and it can be assumed that the mages brought with them escorts, apprentices, and others to assist on their mission. It is, however, known that their leader was a mage named Tal Rasha. From every account I have read, he was a paragon of the Horadrim, a selfless and noble leader who held the order together through many of its darkest hours.

Taking shards of the Worldstone itself, Tyrael fashioned three soulstones, each imbued with the power to contain the essence of a Prime Evil. Jered Cain recounts that Mephisto's soulstone was sapphire, Baal's was amber, and Diablo's was ruby, or blood-hued. He also says that an intelligent and pious mage named Zoltun Kulle was given the task of carrying the stones and capturing the demons' souls within them, for that task most suited him. Though it is not explicitly stated, we can assume that Zoltun Kulle was a mage of the highest order within the Ennead mage clan, almost certainly a master of alchemy, alteration, and transmutation.

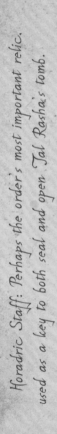

Horadric Staff: Perhaps the order's most important relic, used as a key to both seal and open Tal Rasha's tomb.

Horadric Malus:
Used by the Horadrim to forge enchanted armaments for their struggles against the Prime Evils. Later entrusted to the Sisterhood of the Sightless Eye.

Before the Horadrim's founding, the Prime Evils had been spreading terror, hatred, and destruction among humankind for many years. It is known that the Primes possessed the uncanny ability to inhabit the living bodies of humans, possibly even assuming the identities of political and religious figures to deceive and twist Kehjistan's populace. Fortunately for the Horadrim, the soulstones were attuned to the demons' vile essences, allowing the mages to track down the Primes even when their true forms were hidden within mortal shells.

Ironically, it was Mephisto, the Lord of Hatred, believed to be the most intelligent of the Prime Evils, who was found and captured first in or around one of the great urban centers of Kehjistan. The fight cost many innocent lives, and the Horadrim vowed to avoid confronting another Prime Evil in a populated area. Once Mephisto's essence was trapped, his soulstone was given to the emergent order of the Zakarum (discussed in depth later in this tome) by Tal Rasha, who knew that only they could be trusted with such a grim responsibility. Years later, the Zakarum would build the Temple City of Travincal in that same area, in the jungles near Kurast, in order to protect the soulstone. This would, of course, have dire consequences, as Mephisto's hatred would corrupt that noble religion over time.

The task of hunting the Primes was a daunting one, and the mages were undoubtedly confounded on many occasions, losing the demons' trail before picking up on it again.

Horadric Cube: A miraculous device that works via the principles of transmutation and alchemy. The Horadrim preserved important artifacts and equipment by separating them into their component parts for future use. By later utilizing these elements with the cube, they could reassemble the original item.

In time, Diablo and Baal journeyed west over the Twin Seas to the deserts of Aranoch. The Horadrim remained in close pursuit. Baal took refuge inside the city of Lut Gholein for three days while Tal Rasha and the Horadrim patiently waited. The demon lord then fled north into the scorched wasteland. The harsh desert did not protect him from the Horadrim, for they were men as tenacious as they were prodigious in magic.

The Lord of Destruction unleashed the fury of his powers upon them. The land exploded and fire erupted from the broken earth, burning everything and everyone in its path. The ground fell away, and the combatants plummeted into a network of subterranean caverns. Still, the indomitable Horadrim pressed the attack.

In a desperate attempt to survive, Baal hurled a devastating spell at Tal Rasha, shattering the Amber Soulstone. Nevertheless, the men fought on and subdued the raging demon lord. Tal Rasha, gathering the largest of the soulstone's shards, trapped Baal's destructive essence within it.

It should be noted that there is some controversy about how the Amber Soulstone was shattered. Even the studious Vizjerei mage Nor Tiraj has conflicting accounts in different documents about how this came to be. Yet another account, from a different source, states that it was the inability of one of the Horadrim in particular, Zoltun Kulle, to properly handle the stone in battle that led to its breaking. Whatever the case, when Baal had been drawn into the shard, it became clear that the fragment by itself could not contain his essence forever.

In a profound moment of insight, it was Zoltun Kulle who suggested that a human might be able to contain the demon's essence, using the shard as a conduit to his body. Kulle believed that a mortal heart would serve as a kind of surrogate soulstone. When he said that they would need a mortal vessel to bind Baal within, to wrestle the demon for all eternity, a silence fell over the mages. An instant later, it was Tal Rasha himself, their beloved leader, who stepped forward to make the awful sacrifice.

Jered Cain's notes suggest that Tyrael then appeared and whispered to Tal Rasha, "Your sacrifice will be long remembered, noble mage." He then led the men through the subterranean tunnels into the burial chambers of long-dead kings.

There, deep within one of the largest tombs, the Horadrim built a binding stone etched with runes of containment, held fast to the chamber's walls by unbreakable chains. Tal Rasha then ordered his brethren to chain him to the stone. As the other mages looked on in sorrow, Tyrael approached and jammed the golden shard into Tal Rasha's heart, transferring Baal's essence into the mage's body. Sorrowfully, the Horadrim sealed the chamber and left their brother behind to wrestle with Baal's writhing spirit, presumably for all eternity.

With the loss of Tal Rasha, Jered Cain became the leader of the Horadrim. He and his surviving brethren followed Diablo's trail of terror for nearly a decade. Their hunt took them to the distant western lands of Khanduras, where Diablo was finally confronted and ultimately imprisoned within the Crimson Soulstone. This time, the soulstone worked properly and the demonic essence of the Lord of Terror was trapped. The stone was then hidden within a labyrinthine cave system near the river Talsande.

Tyrael appeared before the Horadrim a final time and commended them for having achieved so great but so bitter a victory. He declared that the site must be guarded for all time, lest the Lord of Terror someday walk once more among men.

The Horadrim who remained built a small monastery and a system of catacombs within the caves. There was much debate as to what the order should do at this point, having received no further guidance from Tyrael. Jered commanded that records be kept. Rules of conduct were devised, and the rudimentary formalization of the Horadrim order began in earnest.

Yeah. I am aware of the texts which state that Tal Rasha offered this suggestion, but after much research, I believe Kulle's role here was downplayed for reasons that will become more obvious when you read "The Hunt for Zoltun Kulle."

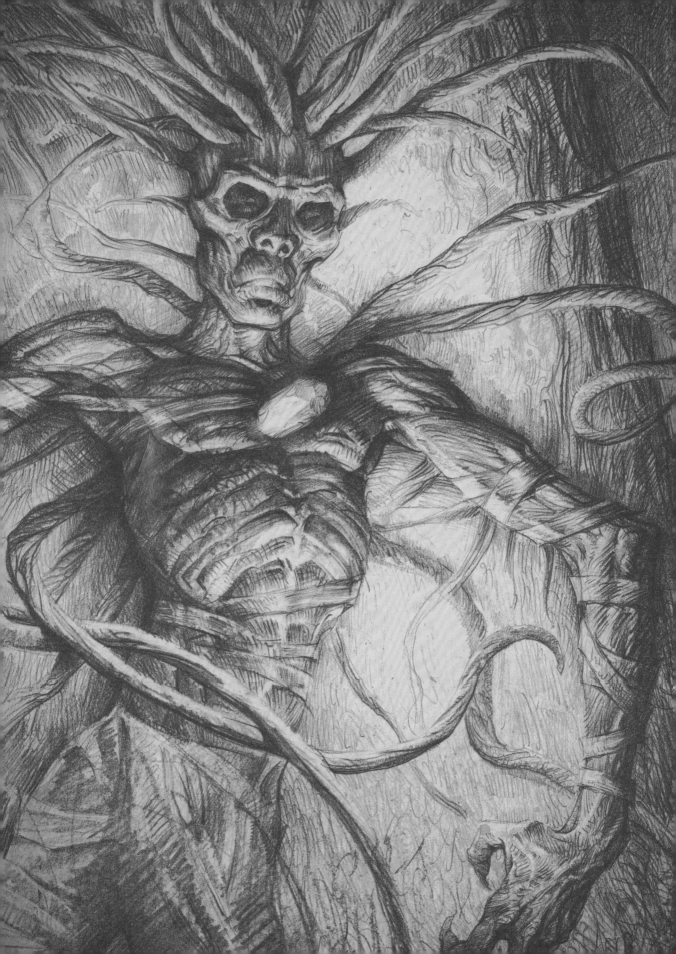

It can then be presumed that some returned to the homes they had left so long before, while others continued to carry out their dire mission, seeking out evil in its many incarnations and standing as guardians against the forces of darkness. Regardless, the fundamental nature of the Horadrim order changed at this time as its members transitioned from being a diverse band of warrior mages to a society of stoic academics.

One exception, of course, was Zoltun Kulle. To better understand the tragic story of this once-great mage, I have included a treatise on the subject written by Jered Cain himself:

THE HUNT FOR ZOLTUN KULLE

Following our capture of the Three, Zoltun Kulle took leave of the Horadrim and returned to Kehjistan to pursue his studies of magic. We heard little of him in subsequent years until disturbing reports flooded in that he had built a sprawling archive beneath the eastern deserts and begun a number of strange and unholy experiments.

Initially, we did not know what to make of these reports, but then we learned the true depth of Kulle's madness . . .

The Hunt for the Three had left Kulle a hollow and unfeeling shell of a man. He felt no pleasure or pain, anticipation or regret. He had become obsessed with soulstones, and believed that he could create one of his own—a vessel capable of harnessing the essences of both angels and demons. Zoltun Kulle would then use this Black Soulstone, filled with rage and hope, fear and valor, as a substitute for his own black and empty heart.

Though it pained us greatly, we agreed that our former friend had to die before he could complete his twisted goal.

I will say nothing of how the killing of Kulle took place, and who accomplished it, for that is among the greatest secrets of our order. After the deed was done, two more of his archives were found in the deserts and oases; we destroyed them. While the unfortunate affair of Zoltun Kulle did not extinguish the fire of the Horadrim, the flame never burned so brightly again.

Fortunately, I have never come across evidence that any other members of the order suffered a fate similar to Kulle's. In fact, what became of the other mages is somewhat of a mystery, but it is known that as time passed, the Horadrim's numbers dwindled. It must be understood that the Horadrim were always an extremely secretive society of ascetics.

In my own family, I can see that every generation I know of has been one of scholars and educators, as at some point the mantle of Horadric champion was removed. Regardless, I am convinced that the knowledge passed down from those distant times might well save us from the coming darkness.

The Rise of Zakarum

In the centuries following the Mage Clan Wars, the pendulum between mysticism and faith swung heavily toward the latter. Humankind had seen the disastrous consequences of magic, and while these arts were still practiced by some, the majority began turning to faith as a foundation for their lives.

This atmosphere gave rise to myriad religions, but none have moved and shaped history so much as the Zakarum Church. From my research, it appears that the seeds of this faith were planted by a mysterious figure named Akarat at some point prior to the formation of the Horadrim.

By the accounts I hold to be true, Akarat was a wandering ascetic from the rugged mountain island of Xiansai, north of Kehjistan. Having become disillusioned with society and its incessant conflicts, he joined the ranks of a humble meditative order that sought enlightenment and peace in Xiansai's high, snowy peaks.

One night, while deep in meditation, he envisioned a spectacular flash of light and energy cascading across the sky. With this phenomenon came insight regarding the universe, reality, and humankind itself as an ascended power. Akarat attributed his revelation to an angelic being named Yaerius, or "son of light" in his native language.

Subsequently, Akarat wrote extensively about the role of humans as powerful beings of Light meant to bring alignment to all things in the universe. All men and women, he purported, were bound together in a spectrum of cosmic radiance that was the foundation of existence itself.

Moved by what he saw, Akarat set out on a grand journey to the ancient cities of Kehjistan, intent on enlightening his fellow man about the divine Light that existed within everyone, no matter what their race, religion, or social status. He is said to have exuded selflessness and compassion in their purest forms. Over time, a number of loyal disciples flocked to Akarat's side.

By all accounts, Akarat was kind, selfless, and unassuming. What I find most interesting is that he never desired that his teachings would lead to the formation of a religion. His goal was simple: to share the wondrous things he had learned so that others could live with goodness in their hearts.

At some point—the lore varies on the date—Akarat disappeared into the jungles of Kehjistan, content that he had spread his message to as many others as he could. He was never seen again.

Over the following years, his ideals were carried on and preached in the streets of Kehjistan's cities by a devout few. The name Zakarum came into use to describe those who followed the ideal of Zakara, or "inner Light." Akarat himself had never given a name to his beliefs, for he had never intended them to represent an actual institution. The appearance of this name, however, represents that the Zakarum faithful were becoming more of a formal group.

When the Horadrim captured Mephisto's wretched essence within the Sapphire Soulstone, the mages turned to the Zakarum believers, who were at that time still a small and humble order, for assistance. Tal Rasha, in particular, had an affinity with the faith's monks, and he firmly believed that they were the only individuals who could be trusted with guarding the soulstone.

My own explanation for Akarat's supernatural experience differs from historical accounts. Ever since the end of the Sin War, there have been rare reports of mystics witnessing what I can only describe as Uldyssian's ultimate sacrifice and merger with the universe. Descriptions in the *Books of Kalan* note that the sudden release of his energies illuminated the sky quite brilliantly. I believe that this act still echoes throughout time—albeit on a psychic plane rather than a physical one—and can be seen only by those deep in meditation. Thus, I theorize that it is this phenomenon that Akarat witnessed and interpreted as the being Yaerius.

As the Horadrim continued their hunt for the remaining Primes, the Zakarum set about building a temple where they could safeguard Mephisto's soulstone. It was in the dense jungles near Kurast that they ultimately founded what became known as Travincal. This humble place of worship would later grow into a massive temple city at the heart of eastern civilization.

Much of what came to pass in the generations that followed has been written about extensively, and is no mystery to those of us now living in modern times. In summation, the Zakarum order grew ever more influential until it became the supreme political power in all of Kehjistan. The faith's leaders codified their beliefs and created a religious hierarchy composed of differing offices. The holy seat of the Que-Hegan, the highest divine authority of the church, was established and filled. Under this revered figure, attendant archbishops of the High Council were tasked with administering the various territories under Zakarum control.

With Kehjistan under its heel, the church looked to what some saw as the barbaric and uncivilized regions of the west. Rakkis, a devout champion of the faith, marshaled a great host to claim and enlighten these lands in the name of the Que-Hegan. His long and arduous crusade to colonize the west would modernize many of these lands, in some cases through brute force. Rakkis finally settled in Westmarch, which was named to commemorate his grand crusade, and reigned as king of that region until the end of his days.

Following the conquest, regional lords from the east were appointed to govern these new outlying hubs in the name of the Zakarum Church. With that, the faith's reach had spread to nearly every corner of the world, leaving only a scarce few regions untouched by its influence.

Trag'Oul: A guardian of Sanctuary, by most accounts, aligned with neither the Heavens nor the Hells. Although information is scarce, he reportedly aided Uldyssian and the edyrem during the Sin War, intent on keeping our world free from both angelic and demonic influences.

The *Books of Kalan* describe this mysterious entity as a celestial dragon whose body resembles a constellation of stars.

Modern History

The Darkening of Tristram

It would be impossible to tell the tale of the present age without writing about the troubled town of Tristram. Located in a remote province known as Khanduras, far from the bustling cities of the east, or even the rain-drenched ports of Westmarch, Tristram played a central role in the unfolding peril of our times.

Indeed, having lived in Tristram all my life, and having been witness to the dark events chronicled here, I still have difficulty believing that my home became the center of so much strife and fear. But I digress . . .

As mentioned in earlier accounts, the Horadrim built their monastery atop the cave system containing Diablo's soulstone. Over time, those first Horadrim settled the land and founded Tristram. As the town grew, other farmers and settlers made the surrounding region their home as well.

Long years passed, and Tristram prospered, though its population never exceeded a few dozen families. None who lived there, under the shadow of the Horadric monastery, ever suspected that Terror itself slept beneath their quiet town.

More than two centuries later, the Zakarum lord Leoric arrived, and Tristram began to take on significance in regional affairs. My knowledge of Leoric's origins comes from my own observations as well as his private journals, which describe how he traveled from Kehjistan and, at the behest of the Zakarum Church, declared himself Khanduras' king.

Acting on counsel from his trusted adviser, Archbishop Lazarus, Leoric established his seat of power in Tristram. Upon his arrival, the king began turning the sleepy town into a regional capital. The Horadric monastery at that time was abandoned and largely in ruins. Leoric converted the ancient structure into a grand Zakarum cathedral, unaware of the vast labyrinth and catacombs the Horadrim had built beneath it.

Initially, the people of Khanduras were wary of their foreign ruler, but I can attest to the fact that Leoric was a wise and just king who exemplified the greatest virtues of the Zakarum. In time, he won the hearts and minds of his subjects, which makes the events that ended his reign all the more tragic.

After years of idyllic peace and quiet, and for reasons then unknown, Leoric's countenance began to darken. The king became irrational at first, but soon began to show the signs of madness and paranoia. It was only when Leoric declared war against the neighboring kingdom of Westmarch that we began to see just how far our king had fallen.

Those close to the king tried to convince him that the war was both unjust and unwinnable. But Lazarus, always Leoric's closest confidant, convinced him that Westmarch was plotting against him. In his paranoia, Leoric sent the meager army of Khanduras into battle. His eldest son, Aidan, seeking his father's approval, joined the forces as well.

Soon after the army's departure, Leoric's youngest son, Albrecht, went missing. Already in the throes of madness, the king raged at the loss of his beloved boy. Convinced either by delusion or by very real specters (who can say?), Leoric became certain that the townsfolk had conspired against him and his family, and he tortured and executed many innocent citizens in an attempt to discern Albrecht's whereabouts. Because of his erratic and cruel actions, the once-gentle Leoric became known as the Black King.

Lachdanan, the captain of Leoric's knights, returned from the war in Westmarch with only a few ragged survivors and found his cherished kingdom in disarray and his fellow citizens gripped by terror. Angered by these events, he confronted Leoric, but the king's madness engulfed him fully, and Leoric ordered his guards to kill Lachdanan and his men.

So it was that Lachdanan and his fellow knights were forced to slay their maddened king. However, before he expired, Leoric put a curse on his slayers. Lachdanan and his men nonetheless thought to honor the noble ruler Leoric had once been and give him a proper burial in the tombs beneath the cathedral. What became of them, I do not know for certain, but I have been told that Lachdanan's damned soul eventually found peace.

Soon, even greater tragedy befell our poor town. More and more citizens disappeared; livestock were mysteriously butchered in the fields; and rumors of horrific creatures prowling the night spread like wildfire. Worse still were the audible screams that could be heard late at night, echoing from the depths of the cathedral.

With Leoric dead and Lachdanan missing, the townsfolk turned to Archbishop Lazarus for assurance. Lazarus, who had been missing for some time, had returned to report that he himself had been ravaged and taken into the catacombs beneath the cathedral by what he could only describe as demons.

In his terrified ramblings, he reminded everyone that Prince Albrecht was still missing, but suggested that the boy might be alive, held captive by the insidious denizens of the labyrinth. Seemingly obsessed with rescuing the young prince, Lazarus led many of the townspeople down into the catacombs, unfortunates who were never to be seen again.

Amidst the chaos, I began to realize that the horrific creatures that wandered Tristram by night reminded me of ones I had read about in the old Horadric tomes passed down to me by my family. As I scoured those tales of angels, demons, and the Horadrim again, I came to a stunning realization: All those stories I had dismissed as myth and legend were true.

Although humbled, I was also filled with a sense of purpose. I knew then that I possessed knowledge that could be used to fight Tristram's corruption. From that day forward, I vowed to arm whomever I could with enough wisdom and information to defeat the evil that had arisen.

In those bleak and unforgiving times, many townspeople would gather at night at the Tavern of the Rising Sun. They sought to take comfort in the company of others, as well as the calming effects of Tristram ale. It was then that the crossroads of life led me to a woman known as Adria, a witch who had just recently come to Tristram for reasons unbeknownst to me. Adria, a vendor of potions and scrolls, was quite an intriguing woman. She was also very resourceful in collecting rare artifacts and arcana. I found her knowledge about mysticism and demonology most valuable, though I found her behavior to be peculiar at times.

We spent many nights poring over the history of the Horadrim and the Hunt for the Three. At that time, having immersed myself in their lore, I began to see myself as one of them. Indeed, perhaps I was the last of the Horadrim. Though it seems naive now, it took me quite a long period to come to the conclusion that the Darkening of Tristram was directly caused by the secret evil the Horadrim had buried so long ago: Diablo, the Lord of Terror.

Meanwhile, as rumors of the horrific events in Tristram spread, mercenaries and adventurers came from all over the world to test their mettle and seek their fortune in the labyrinth beneath the cathedral.

It was at this time that Prince Aidan finally returned to Tristram from his battles against Westmarch, seeking the solace of his home. Like Lachdanan before him, he was horrified by what he learned had befallen his father and his younger brother.

Tempered by war and loss, Aidan vowed to rescue Albrecht and banish the foul demonic power that had gripped Leoric's kingdom. So it was that he ventured into the catacombs beneath the ruined cathedral to find his missing brother.

He was not alone in this task. Of the numerous adventurers who had been drawn to Tristram, the most valorous joined Aidan's side. One was a rogue from the Sisterhood of the Sightless Eye, a mysterious organization headquartered in the mountains east of Tristram. (I will discuss this group later.) She was well versed in the arts of ranged combat and possessed an uncanny ability to sense and disarm traps.

Another was a Vizjerei sorcerer from the lands of Kehjistan who had been sent by his elders to observe the dark happenings in Tristram. As I soon learned, the mage also had an interest in discovering lost tomes and magical artifacts that might be hidden away in the vast labyrinth beneath the town.

In addition to the rogue and the sorcerer, there were others who, like Aidan, were warriors trained in all manner of weapons and armor. These combatants embodied strength and resilience but had little to no knowledge of magic.

Beneath the cathedral, Aidan and these other champions encountered many horrors. He and his band quickly dispatched a bloated and grotesque demon who called himself the Butcher.

The heroes also discovered that Leoric had been resurrected as the grotesque Skeleton King, bound to Diablo's dark will. Witnessing the reanimated visage of his father was a harrowing encounter for Aidan, made even more heartbreaking by the fact that he was forced to strike him down.

Our town blacksmith, Griswold, described the gruesome Butcher to me in great detail, much to my dismay.

A lesser man might have given up then, but not Aidan. After returning to recount the tale, he braved the cathedral's depths once again in the hope that his brother was still alive. Instead of returning with any sign of his brother, however, Aidan came back with the staff of Lazarus. According to Aidan, the Zakarum archbishop had long deceived Leoric and Tristram's populace. At the time, I did not know quite what to make of Aidan's claim, but after those terrible events I would uncover the truth surrounding the full conspiracy.

Lazarus had been one of the keepers tasked with watching over Mephisto's soulstone in Travincal, the heart of the Zakarum empire in Kurast. As I would later learn, Mephisto had extended his influence beyond the confines of the stone. Over centuries, he had corrupted the highest echelons of the Zakarum faithful.

Due in large part to Mephisto's influence, Lazarus had convinced Leoric to take on the position as Khanduras' king and establish his seat of power in the unassuming town of Tristram.

Upon arriving here, Lazarus released the evil from beneath the cathedral by allowing Diablo's essence to escape from its soulstone. The Lord of Terror had then attempted to possess Leoric, but had succeeded only in driving the king mad. What is most despicable, though, is that it was Lazarus who had kidnapped Prince Albrecht and taken him deep into the catacombs at Diablo's bidding.

Aidan and his comrades continued battling through the subterranean tombs, clashing with ever more powerful foes. As news of their exploits grew less frequent, I began to fear that they had encountered Diablo himself and failed.

Then, without warning, I heard what could only have been the death cry of Diablo. Aidan emerged from the bowels of the cathedral, coated in his own blood and all manner of demonic ichor. The terrible screams emanating from the catacombs stopped. Of the demons that had wandered the areas surrounding Tristram, there was no further sign.

That is when I realized that young Aidan and his brave companions had done the impossible: They had triumphed over Diablo, the Lord of Terror.

The Dark Wanderer

It was a dismal time following the horrors of Diablo's rise and the Darkening of Tristram. I longed to know the truth of what happened in the final hours before the horrors were ended, but the man who emerged from beneath the cursed cathedral was not the same courageous warrior who had ventured into the catacombs to rescue his brother.

Aidan increasingly shunned the company of others. He spent his days in isolation and roamed the streets at night, seemingly without direction or purpose. Indeed, the witch Adria appeared to be the only person capable of offering comfort to Aidan during this sorrowful period. As the rest of the town struggled to recover in the aftermath of Diablo's reign of terror, Aidan and Adria spent long nights behind closed doors.

Tristram had become a quiet and sleepy hamlet once again. Tales had spread across Sanctuary of the town that had drawn the bravest adventurers in the world, like flies to the spider's web, only to meet their doom.

It was many days after Aidan's harrowing journey to save his brother that the haunted warrior spoke to me. He confided in me the truth then of what he had faced in the lowest depths of the catacombs: Aidan and the adventurers who had survived to the end found themselves in an area the broken young man described as "the threshold of Hell itself."

There they had encountered the most fearful abomination of any they had yet faced: Diablo—a nightmare incarnate, a terrifying horned demon the color of blood. They battled desperately, but the struggle was not merely physical: The demon forced Aidan to relive his worst nightmares, his greatest failures, and his fears that he would never live up to the expectations of his father. But, convinced that he might still save his brother, Aidan fought through the worst of what Diablo inflicted. The group of adventurers wore the demon down, and ultimately it was Aidan who delivered the killing blow—only to watch the abomination shift before his very eyes into the form of his young brother, Albrecht. Diablo had possessed the boy's body and twisted it into a physical representation of living Terror.

I can only imagine that Aidan's mind was shattered upon realizing that he had killed his only brother. When Aidan finished his recounting, he whispered several times, "I thought I could contain it. I thought I could contain it." He went on to mumble a number of other disturbing things, including something about his "brothers" awaiting him in the east. I knew Aidan was troubled by what he had experienced, and at the time I interpreted what he said as meaningless ramblings.

The next day Aidan was gone. I spoke with Adria soon after his departure and learned that the warrior had traveled east to seek out mystics who might exorcise the waking nightmare that plagued him.

As I meditate back on those days, there is much I would have liked to have asked of Aidan and Adria before they left, as well as many others in town. Unfortunately, such a confused and fetid air hung upon the world back then that I was not thinking clearly. Nor, I suspect, were any of the other remaining citizens of Tristram.

Although I did not succumb, as did so many others, to the wave of insanity that swept the land, I did receive a wound to my spirit that I have not recovered from to this day. Dark thoughts always live at the edges of my mind, like vultures awaiting a feast.

I must now, regrettably, tell of the most troubling time of my life. It was mere weeks after Diablo's defeat that Tristram fell once again to demons.

It was only after the town was utterly destroyed and nearly all those who remained were slaughtered and raised from the dead that I myself was taken prisoner. We had no indication where the demons had come from, but even in my weakened state I surmised that the cause of their appearance was to ensure that no able-bodied combatants were left alive to follow Aidan into the east.

It was then that a horrifying realization dawned on me as I recalled Aidan's words: "I thought I could contain it." Could it be that Aidan was wrestling with the spirit of Diablo himself? And if so, what were his true intentions in going east?

Regardless, the most important piece in all of this is that I survived, and I did so thanks to the efforts of a handful of brave and noble individuals. They had been made aware of my plight and the hellish creatures assailing Tristram.

Many had traveled from the far corners of the world—among them a noble paladin of the Zakarum, a brooding necromancer from the eastern jungles, a powerful amazon from the Skovos Isles, an enigmatic sorceress from Kehjistan, and a mighty barbarian from the slopes of Mount Arreat itself! Together they fought with courage such as I had rarely seen, and ultimately they saved me from the jaws of death.

Shortly after Aidan's departure, Adria set out as well. I am, of course, aware of many things now that I did not know then: that Adria took Gillian the barmaid with her to Caldeum; that when Adria left, she was pregnant with you, dear Leah; and that she gave birth to you in Caldeum and left you there in Gillian's care.

The period of my imprisonment is a time that is brought back to me on cold, damp nights when my wounds scream again from the torment. Remembering it is like looking back to a fitful night of sleep when one nightmare is layered upon another. At the time, the dreams seem make sense, but they then dissolve into nonsense as you meditate on them in the light of day. Finally, all that is left are images of the nightmare and a sickly feeling which invades your days as if something were very wrong. Gentle, indeed, is the protection within us that does not allow fo the memory of pain. If I were to clearly remember, or be able to feel the pain I went through at that time, I doubt I would possess enoug sanity to write this document.

My greatest concern, however, was not for my own well-being. I quickly shared with the heroes my true fear: that Diablo, lurking within Aidan's tortured soul, was guiding the troubled warrior to release the other two Prime Evils that the Horadrim had imprisoned so long ago. For if Aidan released both Baal and Mephisto, humankind would surely suffer an age of darkness and despair beyond imagining. With this, then, in mind, I convinced the group of champions to travel eastward to intercept Aidan and thwart Diablo's plans.

Early on in Aidan's journey, he had crossed paths with an unfortunate soul named Marius. Much of what I know now regarding the events I am about to convey, I retrieved from the remains of a cell within a burned-out sanitarium in Westmarch. (More on this location will be detailed later.) It was there that Marius, his mind shattered from the time he had spent with Aidan, had carved the accounts of his experience into the floor of his cell with his own fingernails. Fortunately, these writings were still legible despite the damages to Marius' room.

Which I speak of in "The Hunt for the Three."

During this time, I referred to Aidan as the Dark Wanderer. After his departure from Tristram, he sought passage to the eastern port of Lut Gholein. Passing through the Eastgate Monastery, Aidan encountered the Sisters of the Sightless Eye, many of whom had recently been corrupted by the Maiden of Anguish, Andariel. As with the other demons who invaded Tristram, Andariel had arrived to prevent Aidan's pursuers from interfering with the Wanderer's dire mission.

The Sisterhood of the Sightless Eye is a most intriguing organization. Its origins are rooted deeply in the history of the Askari who dwell on the Skovos Isles. From the earliest days of their culture, the Askari held in their possession an artifact known as the Sightless Eye, a mirror which served as a window to perceive the future. The Sisterhood of the Sightless Eye, a group of amazon dissidents, stole the artifact and fled, ultimately occupying Eastgate Keep. Whether Andariel came to possess the Eye, or, if she did not, what became of it, is unknown.

I speculate now that following the Dark Exile and the Prime Evils' banishment, Andariel (and her twin, Duriel, as we shall see) concluded that the Primes would inevitably use the innate powers of man to reclaim the Burning Hells. Therefore, they endeavored to gain favor with the Lord of Terror by protecting his human host.

In any case, the mighty champions who liberated me from my prison soon faced the Maiden of Anguish. She struck at them physically, but battered them emotionally as well, stirring within each of them memories of loss, sadness, betrayal, and regret—feeding on their angst and relishing their despair. Despite the heavy toll on the minds of those she attacked, however, the hunters succeeded in dispatching Andariel after a long and hard-fought battle.

Though the Maiden of Anguish had not succeeded in killing Aidan's pursuers, she was successful in one respect: She bought the Dark Wanderer time to reach his destination.

After traversing the arid deserts of Aranoch, the heroes arrived at Lut Gholein, hot on the Wanderer's heels. It wasn't until they reached the very tombs where the mage Tal Rasha wrestled the demon lord Baal that they finally cornered their prey.

There, within Tal Rasha's chamber, the group was faced with Duriel, the Lord of Pain—who, like his sister, had pledged his loyalty to Diablo. Duriel exacted a heavy toll upon the heroes, savoring the agonized screams of the wounded. Though hopelessly fatigued, both mentally and physically, the mortal champions overcame the Maggot King, slaying him as they had his sister. But again, time was of the essence.

As the heroes arrived at Tal Rasha's tomb, they realized they were too late to prevent Baal's release. To their amazement, Tyrael himself was present. He had arrived there and grappled with Aidan, hoping to prevent him from liberating Baal. Through some means of cruel manipulation, Baal had convinced Marius to remove the amber shard lodged in Tal Rasha's body, thus freeing him. Aidan and Tal Rasha, the latter then fully controlled by Baal, turned their combined might on Tyrael.

Knowing that he would not prevail against his foes, the archangel of Justice had ordered Marius to take Baal's stone into the Burning Hells and shatter it within the Hellforge. (I will describe this mysterious place in further depth later.) As the cowering mortal departed the tomb, Aidan and Tal Rasha overwhelmed Tyrael.

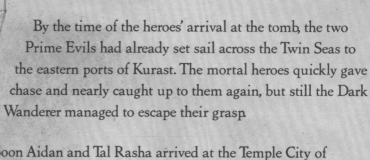

By the time of the heroes' arrival at the tomb, the two Prime Evils had already set sail across the Twin Seas to the eastern ports of Kurast. The mortal heroes quickly gave chase and nearly caught up to them again, but still the Dark Wanderer managed to escape their grasp.

Soon Aidan and Tal Rasha arrived at the Temple City of Travincal—then held to be the holiest site of Zakarum. It was there, deep within the bowels of the magnificent temple, that Mephisto's Sapphire Soulstone was kept.

As mentioned earlier in my writings, many of the greatest Zakarum paladins and their commanders had already been corrupted by Mephisto's vile influence long before Aidan and Tal Rasha arrived. It has even been documented that Sankekur, the Que-Hegan, or Supreme Patriarch of the Zakarum Church, had fallen under Mephisto's control.

This much is certain: Not everyone at the temple was corrupt, and Travincal was easily the most heavily guarded site in all of Kehjistan. Regardless, the Wanderer would not be denied. Eyewitness reports suggest that many of the temple's defenders fell prey to overwhelming fear and fled the complex altogether. Additional reports suggest that many more turned against each other, further decimating the Zakarum's ranks. These accounts undoubtedly evidence the influence of the Lords of Terror and Destruction.

Ultimately, the Wanderer and Tal Rasha made their way into the temple's innermost chamber, where Mephisto's soulstone was kept. There, they released Mephisto, who quickly took physical possession of the holy Que-Hegan. The tortured body of the Zakarum leader transformed into the hideous visage of Mephisto's demonic form. And thus, after nearly three centuries apart, the Prime Evils were united once again.

Within that chamber, the Primes devised a final stratagem to retake the Burning Hells and claim vengeance upon those who overthrew them. This included their long-sought goal to corrupt the Worldstone, thereby enslaving all of humankind and its nephalem potential to their will. With an army of nephalem as their vanguard, the Primes would quickly overwhelm the Hells' traitorous legions and reestablish their infernal reign for all time.

To accomplish this, the Primes combined their powers to open a portal that would allow them access to their former domain. It was then that Diablo finally cast off the mortal visage of Prince Aidan, and assumed his true demonic form.

Intent on rallying the legions within Hell still loyal to the Three, Diablo crossed through the shimmering portal. Baal began his long journey north to corrupt the Worldstone, while Mephisto alone remained, bent on destroying any and all opposition to their plan.

When the mortal heroes arrived in Kurast, the city had already been overrun by demonic hordes. Bloody combat was waged in the streets as the heroes fought to gain entrance into Travincal. Once inside, they faced not only demons but also the corrupted zealots and High Council members of the Zakarum faith. At the time, I doubt it occurred to the champions that they were toppling the world's greatest religion, but such was the case. Nonetheless, they continued down into the deepest recesses of the temple, where they finally faced Mephisto.

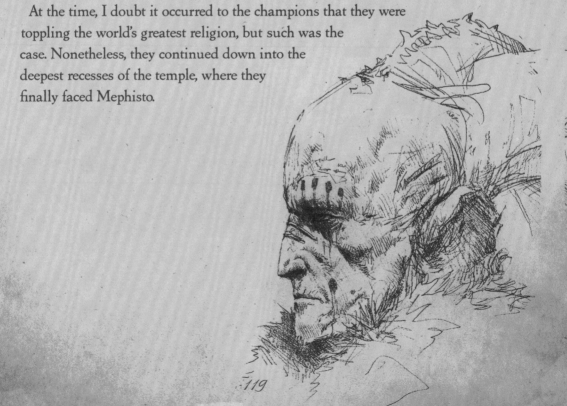

In the fevered combat that ensued, Mephisto worked diligently to turn the hunters' own anger and distrust back against them. But despite the long hunt and the many grueling hours of battle, in the end the heroes defeated Mephisto and trapped his essence within the Sapphire Soulstone.

It was not long after this victory that I arrived to survey the carnage wrought by this terrible conflict. And though it pained me greatly, I knew that the heroes' battle was not over, for if Diablo were to gather an army from the Burning Hells, he would most assuredly return and carry out the Primes' plan despite our efforts.

Those who had fought so hard, for so long, did not hesitate. They drove through the portal without a backward glance, and I . . . I somehow summoned the courage to follow them.

The gateway we entered, however, did not lead directly to Hell. Instead, it allowed access to the breathtaking Pandemonium Fortress, the abandoned bastion that once housed the Worldstone. Even as my senses reeled, I wondered why the Prime Evils had chosen to open a portal there. Perhaps to allow Diablo furtive access into the Hells? Whatever the case, it meant that perhaps there was still time.

The Pandemonium Fortress was the most incredible, astonishing, and perplexing place my mortal eyes have ever beheld. Colors, shapes, textures—none seemed as they should have. My surroundings pulsed and shifted before my eyes. I was overwhelmed, but determined also to offer whatever assistance I might to the heroes who pursued Diablo.

It was then that my eyes fell upon the shining visage of Tyrael. Not wanting to directly intervene and risk the High Heavens learning what had befallen Sanctuary, the archangel regretted that he could not venture into the Hells at the mortals' side. But he offered insight: a theory. A chance, perhaps, to eliminate both Mephisto and Diablo once and for all.

He spoke of the Hellforge, located in the deepest pit of the Realm of Destruction. It was here that the demonic smiths forged Hell's most powerful weapons. Thus, it was said that the dread Hellforge held many unholy anvils, and among them was the Anvil of Annihilation. It was upon this anvil that angelic weapons and artifacts were destroyed. Legends held that anything broken upon the Anvil of Annihilation, no matter how powerful, would be forever negated.

The hunters possessed Mephisto's soulstone already. Tyrael theorized that if they somehow overcame Diablo and trapped his essence as well, then perhaps both soulstones could be shattered upon the anvil. Therefore, in theory, the demon lords themselves would be obliterated and their souls cast into some unseen netherworld.

It is staggering to think back upon that moment. For who could ask such a thing of mere mortals? Tyrael did not have to ask. Without hesitation, the pursuers charged headlong into the fires of the Burning Hells, while Tyrael remained behind to serve as my protector. The champions fought their way across the nightmare landscape and reached the volatile Realm of Destruction, seeking the mythic Hellforge.

I can scarcely imagine what horrors they faced and overcame, but their spirit and will proved indomitable. They stood at the smoldering rim of the Hellforge, and there, upon the Anvil of Annihilation, the heroes shattered Mephisto's soulstone.

The heroes then tracked down Diablo. Despite the odds against them, they succeeded in overtaking the Lord of Terror.

Once again, dear Leah, the sheer tenacity of the human heart proved victorious, for the heroes achieved the impossible: They vanquished Diablo within his own realm. As they pulled the Crimson Soulstone from Diablo's corpse, the demon's massive form began to wither. They set about trapping Diablo's essence within the soulstone, and when they succeeded, Diablo's disintegrating husk took on the form of Prince Aidan.

In honor of the prince's memory, the champions ceremonially wrapped his broken body and threw it into the infernal fires that raged all around them.

With Diablo's soulstone in their possession, the beleaguered heroes made their way back to the Hellforge and sundered the artifact upon the Anvil of Annihilation.

The firsthand accounts of the champions tell us that when both Mephisto's and Diablo's soulstones were shattered, a similar fate befell the Primes. A scream such as no human being had ever heard rent the air, followed by a black and intangible nothingness opening before the heroes. They averted their eyes as the wailing souls of Diablo and Mephisto were swallowed by the yawning darkness.

Upon hearing of this, I remembered the writings of my ancestor Jered Cain, who reported a theory held by Zoltun Kulle: that the spirits of angels and demons could be banished to a place beyond even Heaven and Hell—a place he called the Abyss. When I think back on the champions and their experience at the Hellforge, I know in my bones that Diablo and Mephisto were cast somewhere that would make even them feel fear.

And, though it is morbid, I must be honest and admit that this thought gives me some comfort.

Regardless, with the shattering of the soulstones, yet another chapter in the struggle of humankind against the agents of the Burning Hells had come to an end.

Questions, of course, remained. And years later I would glean the details concerning Aidan and his possession by the Lord of Terror.

It was revealed to me that upon defeating Diablo in the catacombs beneath Tristram, Aidan had thrust the Crimson Soulstone into his own forehead in an effort to trap the essence of Diablo within himself. Now I wonder whether, perhaps, it was Diablo's plan all along to lure the world's greatest champions down into the depths to test their strength and resolve and, in so doing, find the perfect host for his all-devouring evil.

How much of Aidan was in control when he left Tristram, striking out to the east? Was it truly his intention to exorcise the demon from within himself—or was it the voice of Diablo whispering deep in his mind, convincing him that these thoughts were his own? We may never know. But this I tell you, Leah, regarding the final battle with Diablo, when the champions fought him in the midst of the Burning Hells: I now believe, looking back on those events, that a small measure of Aidan remained, fighting the will of Diablo. Perhaps it was not only the heroes who overcame the Lord of Terror, but also Aidan, who contended with the demon from within.

As I say, this is not proven, but simply my belief. And it is beliefs like this which may provide some slim hope, even in the face of ultimate despair.

The Lord of Destruction

As my companions waged their battles against Mephisto and Diablo, Baal set out across the Twin Seas to corrupt the Worldstone, and thereby all of humankind. With the whole of humanity turned to darkness, he would possess an army with a power beyond even that of angels and demons—a fighting force capable of tipping the scales of the Eternal Conflict.

It appears, however, that in order to fulfill his plan, Baal required the Amber Soulstone shard that had been used to imprison him so long ago by the Horadrim. As you will remember from earlier in this tome, the shard had been taken by Marius, the Dark Wanderer's former companion.

Rather than follow Tyrael's orders to destroy the stone, Marius had fled to Westmarch. There, driven to the brink of madness, he had been arrested and confined to a sanitarium. It did not take long for Baal to track him down and acquire the soulstone shard. Reports say that a raging inferno swept through the sanitarium around this time. Sadly, Marius' charred corpse was later found in the remains of the building. I can only assume that this act of destruction was Baal's doing.

For quite some time, I wondered why the soulstone was so vital to Baal's plans, but I believe I now have an adequate explanation. Over the long centuries Baal was imprisoned, the stone became infused with his destructive essence. By melding this Shard of Destruction to the Worldstone, Baal knew that he could irrevocably corrupt the monolithic crystal.

Having secured the shard, Baal marched north from Westmarch, butchering entire villages en route to Mount Arreat. Those who died were not granted peace—they were possessed and transformed into hideous demonic soldiers. By the time Baal reached Arreat, his unholy legions had swelled to number in the thousands.

Some might question why Baal assaulted Arreat in force if he could have reached the Worldstone through stealth and deception. From what I have gathered, every act of mayhem and wanton chaos committed by the demon lord and his minions bolstered the shard's destructive power. Thus, Baal intended to wreak havoc along his journey to ensure that when he reached the Worldstone, the shard itself would be pulsing with untold corruptive energies.

Near Arreat's foothills, Baal contended with the barbarians. These fierce guardians had lived to protect Arreat for generations, believing that the holy "Heart of the World" existed within the mountain. The barbarians had long venerated Bul-Kathos and other nephalem, and they believed that the spirits of these ancients resided upon the lonely peaks of Arreat as a last line of defense against any who would threaten the sacred mount.

By all accounts, the barbarians fought ferociously, living up to their reputation as some of Sanctuary's hardiest warriors. Yet it was not enough to prevent the Lord of Destruction from storming across their lands and sacking their great capital of Sescheron. Eventually, all that stood between Baal and Arreat Summit was Harrogath, a fortress nestled in the mountain's foothills.

Reports suggest that the stronghold's Elders grew desperate at the sight of Baal's marauding armies. To stave off annihilation, they sacrificed themselves to cast an ancient (and forbidden) warding spell, creating a protective barrier around Harrogath.

It was then that Baal's forces laid siege to the bastion. With Tyrael's aid, my brave comrades who had defeated Diablo and Mephisto arrived at Harrogath amidst the chaos.

Over the course of their journey, the heroes' numbers had grown. One newcomer who had pledged herself to the cause was an assassin of the Viz-Jaq'taar, a secretive order created to hunt down and slay renegade sorcerers. Having foresworn the direct use of magic, the assassin donned exotic weapons and armor imbued with elemental energies.

Another newcomer was a druid who traveled far from the fabled woodlands of Scosglen. Prior to meeting this individual, I had read extensively from the ancient druidic tome *Scéal Fada* and knew much about the druids' abilities to command the forces of nature and assume the forms of various beasts.

The band of heroes did all they could to break Baal's demonic siege. Their efforts, however, were overshadowed by treachery. Nihlathak, the only Elder to have survived the warding ritual, believed that unless he made a pact with the Lord of Destruction, his people would be doomed. In exchange for the sparing of Harrogath, the Elder provided Baal with the Relic of the Ancients, one of the holiest artifacts in barbarian culture.

With the artifact in hand, Baal raced up the slopes of Arreat, bypassing the guardian nephalem spirits and breaching the Worldstone's secret chamber within the bowels of the mountain. My allies followed in his tracks, clashing with the demon lord's minions and even proving themselves worthy against Arreat's spectral nephalem. Ultimately, they confronted Baal within the Worldstone's chamber and vanquished him in a ferocious battle that left them at the brink of death.

Yet, as the heroes were horrified to learn, Baal had fused the Shard of Destruction with the Worldstone. All of the strife and horror that had accumulated within the shard had already begun spreading throughout the gargantuan crystal.

When Tyrael arrived to assess the situation, he realized that these dark energies would soon echo through the hearts of all mankind, turning humans irrevocably evil and violent.

And so Tyrael did the unthinkable. He hurled his sword, El'druin, into the Worldstone itself. In that moment, the object over which the Eternal Conflict had been waged—that had created Sanctuary and all its myriad forms of life—was shattered in a horrific explosion.

The Worldstone's destruction was catastrophic. Baal's body was obliterated, and his spirit, I have come to believe, was flung into the Abyss, just like those of the other Primes. What remained of his demonic forces was utterly destroyed as well, and the surrounding area was devastated. To this day, toxic clouds of ash and choking arcane dust hang like a shroud over the land. The decimation was so utterly calamitous that this region is now known as the Dreadlands.

What became of Tyrael after this event is unknown to me, but it is clear that his physical form, like Baal's, was disintegrated. Some fragmented reports suggest that the Sword of Justice, El'druin, survived the explosion and was thrown across the lands of Sanctuary. Rumors tell of a young mortal named Jacob who later wielded the sword and used it to cleanse a curse that had taken hold around his home city of Staalbreak. I hope to confirm these rumors and perhaps write a more detailed account of this series of events in the future.

Think carefully on this, Leah, as recent events surrounding the fallen star have caused me to begin formulating theories which I dare not express here.

Suffice it to say, dear reader, that from the time of Diablo's awakening beneath Tristram to Tyrael's destruction of the Worldstone, the narrative of men, angels, and demons was altered forever. This conflict saw the defeat of five of the seven Lords of Hell. I cannot tell you how significant this is.

For the past twenty years, I have traveled the darkening world and witnessed many things come to pass, waiting to see when these troubles would erupt once again. To be clear, two of the Evils still live—Azmodan, the Lord of Sin, and Belial, the Lord of Lies. The End of Days is coming, and I believe these two will play principal roles in the annihilation of our world.

Also of great concern is a thought that has plagued me for some time: As we have seen, Tyrael is a noble being who has fought on the behalf of our kind time and time again. Yet I am afraid that he is alone in terms of how his fellow angels view humanity. We have witnessed numerous demons and their lords walk this world, but we have heard little of the High Heavens or of the Angiris Council that rules over them. There is something terribly unsettling about Heaven's silence and the unknown role that angels might play in the coming years.

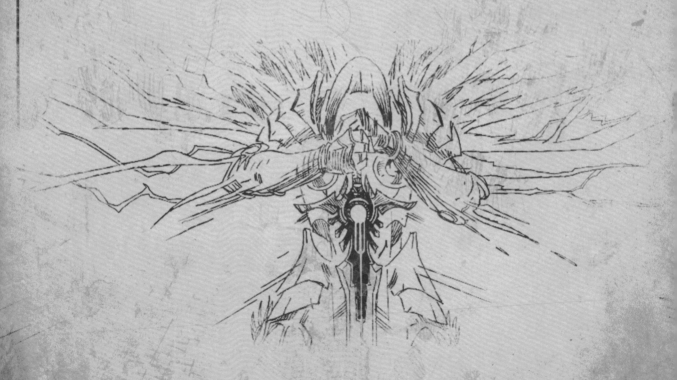

Sanctuary: Lands and Cultures
The Deserts of Aranoch

Since time immemorial, the vast sand-swept deserts of Aranoch have served as a natural barrier between the east and the west. Not until the Zakarum conqueror Rakkis' great crusade was the desert crossed in great numbers. Yet even after traversing and enduring, his forces still had to contend with the nearly impassable Tamoe mountain range that stretches across Aranoch's western border.

Despite the brutal environment, the desert boasts a surprising number of species and robust cultures. The lacuni, or "panther-men," as they are commonly called, are one such example. A number of nomadic human clans also inhabit Aranoch, either living as wandering traders or dwelling temporarily in vast subterranean caverns to escape the desert's oppressive sun.

It is written that the great nation of Ivgorod once controlled the northern reaches of Aranoch as well. The Valley of the Ancient Kings (the site of Tal Rasha's tomb, mentioned earlier in this tome) is said to be a sacred burial ground for some of the ancient Patriarchs who ruled the kingdom. It should be noted that this location was named by Aranoch's inhabitants, not the inhabitants of Ivgorod, and has also been referred to as the Canyon of the Magi (due to an erroneous belief that the mage clans had some part in its creation).

By far, the most important location in Aranoch is the port of Lut Gholein, the Jewel of the Desert. This city's influence throughout history cannot be overstated. Until Rakkis' conquest, much of what those in the east knew about the west was gleaned through Kehjistani merchants who traded in Lut Gholein.

The Dreadlands

This blasted region was once home to the many barbarian tribes and their beloved Mount Arreat, site of the Worldstone. In the course of the Worldstone's destruction, half of Mount Arreat's bulk exploded outward. Now, all that remains is a massive, smoldering crater in the earth.

The aftereffects of the Worldstone's destruction have left a terrible mark upon the realm. Demonic corruption now runs rampant, threatening both man and beast. Tales have spread of phantom horrors and infernal mutations stalking amidst the scarred forestlands, making the Dreadlands a destination shunned by all but the hardiest (or most foolish) of travelers.

No longer charged as caretakers of the sacred mountain, some barbarians have left Arreat behind and struck out to battle evil in atonement for failing in their ancient stewardship. Other tribes have fallen into a state of regression, becoming akin to unreasoning beasts and, in some cases, even cannibals.

One of the only civilized sites left in the Dreadlands is the fortress known as Bastion's Keep. Built long ago by Korsikk, son of Rakkis (see the section on Westmarch), the keep now stands as a bulwark between the violent tribes in the north and the civilized lands to the south. The brave soldiers who guard its walls remain ready to confront any foes—human or otherwise—who might besiege them.

While not native to the region, the secretive cadre of warriors known as the demon hunters has chosen to make its home in the harsh and unforgiving Dreadlands. The abundance of demonic creatures and mutated beasts provides a wealth of training opportunities for the demon hunters to hone their deadly skills.

Entsteig

Located north of the densely forested Sharval Wilds, Entsteig is a proud kingdom that has pledged its loyalties to the Zakarum faith. When Rakkis' army first marched into the western lands centuries ago, he met violent resistance from the peoples of Ivgorod, who viewed his new beliefs as sacrilege. Entsteig, however, opened its gates to Rakkis and embraced his teachings.

Because of its peaceful acceptance of foreign rule, Entsteig quickly modernized and became an important Zakarum territory in the region, much like Westmarch and Khanduras would become. In recent times, many of the most devout Zakarum paladins have hailed from Entsteig.

Due to the thick, mountainous forests that blanket this region, Entsteig developed a culture highly distinct from nearby Ivgorod and the barbarian civilization to the north. The kingdom's inhabitants believe the Sharval Wilds to be an enchanted place of fey spirits, and many old customs and pagan rituals are still practiced there. Even so, these ancient rites have not conflicted with the observance of the Zakarum faith. Rather, Entsteig's people have managed to meld their own esoteric beliefs with their adopted religion.

Ivgorod

Ivgorod is a land steeped in tradition and mystery. It is known as the City of the Patriarchs, and the religious oligarchy rules with an iron fist. The religion of Ivgorod is known as Sahptev and is devoted to the worship of a thousand and one gods and goddesses. This rigidly complex system controls and informs every aspect of Ivgorod's society.

The exotic civilization of Ivgorod once held sway over surrounding lands (such as portions of Entsteig) and the northern deserts of Aranoch. I find it fascinating that some of the ancient rulers of Ivgorod are interred beneath the Valley of the Ancient Kings. But due to Rakkis' crusade, the power of this land was broken. Now, all that remains of this once-great civilization is its snow-capped capital.

The monks of Ivgorod are rarely seen outside of their predominantly isolationist kingdom. Secretive and reclusive, these holy warriors undergo intense mental and physical training to hone their minds and bodies into living instruments of divine justice.

Kehjistan

Perhaps no other region in the world has been so important to shaping human civilization as Kehjistan (known in ancient times as Kehjan). It was here where the mage clans formed and rose to prominence, and where some of the most profound discoveries in science, philosophy, magic, and religion have been made. Following the Sin War millennia ago, Kehjan was renamed Kehjistan to distance itself from that terrible and costly conflict.

The terrain of present-day Kehjistan has changed little over the millennia. Emerald rainforests teeming with life form the bulk of the region. A vast desert known as the Borderlands denotes Kehjistan's northern border, while swamplands lie at its eastern edge.

Kehjistan's capital has changed more than once over the course of its history, due in large part to war and upheaval. By the end of the Mage Clan Wars, the ancient capital of Viz-jun had been reduced to rubble. The city was later rebuilt and, for a time, remained Kehjistan's seat of power. However, the rise of the Zakarum saw the capital move to the church's religious center in Kurast. The capital shifted again more recently after the fall of Travincal (see the previous chapter for my writings on the Dark Wanderer), as the remnants of the Zakarum fled to the trade city of Caldeum.

Known as the Jewel of the East, Caldeum now stands as the center of Kehjistani life and governance. Together with Lut Gholein, it forms what some refer to as "the jewel cities." The Great Library of Caldeum is perhaps the single most important repository of knowledge in the world, and it has been invaluable to me in creating this tome. Despite the decadence and corruption that have befallen the city in recent years, I intend to return there one day and further my studies.

I have heard reports of an underground movement spreading amongst the young pupils of Caldeum's Yshari Sanctum, a legendary facility where many of the present-day mage clans hone their skills. Dissatisfied with their rigid instructors, these rebellious students have taken on the title of wizard (ironic, as it is considered a derogatory term by mages) and sought out dangerous and forbidden magics. They are said to possess the ability to manipulate the primal forces from which reality itself is constructed.

Khanduras

Khanduras is a land bordered by the Gulf of Westmarch to the west and the Tamoe mountain range to the east. It was in these mountains that Rakkis built Eastgate Keep to defend his holdings against the opposing armies of Ivgorod.

The lands of Khanduras are perhaps best known for the events surrounding Diablo's return and the Darkening of Tristram.

In the years following these terrible acts, merchants slowly began to return to the region, looking to profit from adventurers who plumbed the depths beneath Tristram's cathedral. The town of New Tristram arose, but in recent years it has once again fallen to decline.

Scosglen

Scosglen is an untamed verdant wilderness located in the far north of the eastern lands. Here, the druidic culture has lived in harmony with nature since the days of the immortal ancient Vasily. As legend has it, the nephalem led his mortal followers to Scosglen and taught them the *Caoi Dúlra*, a way of life that allowed the druids to bond with their environment.

While the druids have shunned traditional magic, they possess other miraculous skills. Apart from communing with plants and animals, they can take on the forms of certain beasts and, in some rare instances, even bend the forces of nature to their will. Even at the height of their powers, the sorcerers of the mage clans never dared enter Scosglen for fear of the wild and savage powers its inhabitants wielded.

What passes as civilization in Scosglen might seem crude to some, but the druids do not value sprawling urban centers as do Kehjistan's inhabitants. The dwellings of Scosglen consist of ancient stone towers known as druid colleges scattered throughout the region's dense forests. The greatest of these structures is Túr Dúlra, considered the heart of druidic culture. There, it is said that the druids have perfected their synergy with nature for ages beneath the boughs of a magnificent oak tree called Glór-an-Fháidha.

You know this area well. Yeah, but it is important that you know some of the old names and chronology, for these are things that will figure prominently in decoding the end times to come.

The Skovos Isles

Located south of the Western Kingdoms in the Twin Seas, the Skovos Isles consist of four main islands: Philios, Skovos, Lycander, and Skartara. The isles are home to the Askari civilization. Since ancient times, the Askari have espoused a matriarchal form of government, one in which men have a lesser voice and are prohibited from holding the highest offices. In truth, political power is shared between two castes—the warrior amazons and the mystic oracles. Each caste is represented by a queen; thus both queens rule the Skovos Isles in tandem.

The isles are also the origin point of the Sisterhood of the Sightless Eye, exiled rogues who struck out across the world years ago. (I have written more on this group in the chapter concerning the Dark Wanderer.)

The core of Askari mythology revolves around Philios, a first-generation nephalem, and his lover, Lycander, an angelic follower of Inarius. These doomed lovers communicated through an artifact known as the Sightless Eye—which even today is held as one of the most sacred objects in Askari culture.

Legend holds that Philios was a bold and powerful nephalem. The angel Lycander felt drawn to Philios, and the two fell in love. When the demoness Lilith massacred Sanctuary's renegade angels and demons, Lycander fled back to the Heavens. She maintained contact with Philios through an artifact in his possession called the Sightless Eye. In time, however, Lycander's fellow angels discovered she was communing with someone outside the Heavens, though they knew not who it was. Lycander ended the romance and insisted that Philios hide the Eye so that the Heavens would not learn of Sanctuary's existence.

Philios grieved but continued to adventure throughout Sanctuary, and in time met the mortal woman Askarra. The two fell in love, and soon Askarra gave birth to twin girls. The girls grew, hearing tales of the Sightless Eye . . . and they vowed to recover it.

The sisters found the Eye on the island of Skovos, and it was there that they made their home. Though the twins did not use the Eye to communicate with Heaven, they found that they were able to see the future through its mirrored surface. So it was that their culture grew with the Sightless Eye at the heart of their society.

From the more stalwart sister, the amazon caste descended. And from the more ethereal sister, the oracle caste evolved.

The Torajan Jungles

The immense, teeming jungles of Toraja span most of the southwestern expanse of the eastern lands. Even to nearby Kehjistan, this region is a strange and exotic place, filled with vibrant and dangerous flora and fauna that cannot be found anywhere else on Sanctuary.

The verdant Torajan rainforests have cultivated many ancient civilizations, many of which have been lost to the annals of time. The reclusive umbaru tribes of the Teganze forest remain the exception. These groups are said to engage in a highly ritualistic style of warfare in which prisoners willingly submit themselves as sacrifices to honor the revered spirits of the rainforest. The umbaru's overriding belief is that our world is merely a curtain that veils a true reality called Mbwiru Eikura (commonly known as the Unformed Land).

One might ask how the umbaru know the Unformed Land exists if it is hidden from mortal eyes. The answer lies with the tribes' witch doctors, who purportedly can see and experience this otherworldly realm. Witch doctors are fearsome spiritual warriors who have the power to assault both mind and body with dark magics. It has been reported that some witch doctors even possess the ability to summon risen dead creatures to serve them.

Westmarch

Founded by Rakkis, Westmarch was named in honor of the Zakarum warlord's great crusade and marks the farthest western point of his conquest.

Rakkis was loved by the peoples of the west and did much to bring civilization to the surrounding lands, including the building of roads and churches and necessary infrastructure for the burgeoning territories there. In time, Rakkis' heir, Korsikk, continued his father's rule and built Westmarch into a bastion of the Zakarum faith.

Ever wary of attack from the northern barbarians, Korsikk founded the impregnable Bastion's Keep to safeguard all that his father had thought to build.

In the present day, Westmarch is a kingdom that thrives on commerce and maritime trade. Influence from the Zakarum faith has waned of late, and Westmarch is now a forward-looking civilization. Indeed, one might say that it remains one of the healthiest, most vibrant kingdoms left in our troubled world.

Xiansai

Xiansai is a mountainous island nation found in the Frozen Sea at the roof of the world. Due to the isle's insular nature, the Xian have developed a highly distinct culture devoid of major foreign influence. The kingdom distanced itself from the Sin War, the Mage Clan Wars, and other notable conflicts, but it has seen its own share of civil strife.

Historically, many of Xiansai's internal wars have originated from the political maneuvering of the Great Families that hold sway on the island. These wealthy trade groups are said to be constantly competing with one another for influence and power. Each one of these families controls a specific aspect of the kingdom's economy, from its robust fishing industry to the mining of precious metals and gems in the towering Guozhi mountain range.

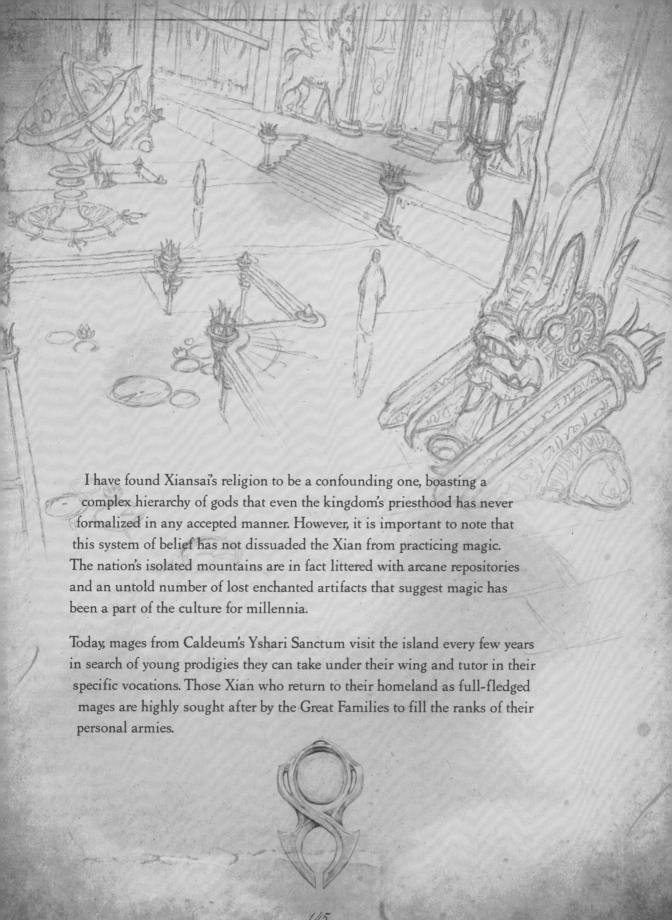

I have found Xiansai's religion to be a confounding one, boasting a complex hierarchy of gods that even the kingdom's priesthood has never formalized in any accepted manner. However, it is important to note that this system of belief has not dissuaded the Xian from practicing magic. The nation's isolated mountains are in fact littered with arcane repositories and an untold number of lost enchanted artifacts that suggest magic has been a part of the culture for millennia.

Today, mages from Caldeum's Yshari Sanctum visit the island every few years in search of young prodigies they can take under their wing and tutor in their specific vocations. Those Xian who return to their homeland as full-fledged mages are highly sought after by the Great Families to fill the ranks of their personal armies.

Dearest Leah,

By now you've no doubt perused this manuscript and gleaned from it at least a cursory knowledge of the dangers that lie in store for our troubled world. Believe me, I know how difficult it is to weigh the balance of these incredible mythologies, how hard it is to believe they could paint a picture of a world even more real and more terrible than the one we now perceive.

I must confess that in the wake of recent events, I have struggled to hold on to hope. When the falling star crashed down and blasted me into the darkened depths of that damned cathedral, I saw my long life flash before my eyes. All at once, I felt the totality of my experience: the unprecedented sights I'd seen, the knowledge I'd accumulated, the pain and loss I'd lived through. And though I was saved from certain death, I feel there was a part of me left behind, still buried beneath that cursed ground.

You would chide me for being morbid, but I cannot shake the feeling that my time is drawing to a close—that death, after all these long years, will finally catch up to me. And thus I hope that my life has had some impact for good in this world, that my work will continue should anything happen to me.

My great desire in leaving this tattered old journal in your possession is that you will take up the challenge of my work when I am gone. It is tedious, to be sure, but like all great works, it may inform the hearts and minds of men in the face of the apocalypse to come. It falls to you now, dear one, to draw your own conclusions regarding these apocryphal texts—and to warn the world of the perils that draw nearer with every passing day.

Oh, Leah, I never wanted any of this for you. I never wanted you to be drawn into the cycle of terror and violence that has hounded me these past twenty years. But fate, it seems, is cruelly fickle. I'm sorry that you must

INSIGHT ⊙ EDITIONS

PO BOX 3088
SAN RAFAEL, CA 94912
WWW.INSIGHTEDITIONS.COM

BLIZZARD ENTERTAINMENT

Text by Flint Dille

Additional Writings: Chris Metzen, Micky Neilson, Matt Burns

Art Direction: Glenn Rane, Doug Gregory, Jeremy Cranford

Additional Art: Trent Kaniuga, John Polidora

Production: Joshua Horst, Kyle Williams, Skye Chandler

Editing: Cate Gary

Lore: Evelyn Fredericksen, Sean Copeland, Justin Parker

Licensing: Matthew Beecher, Jerry Chu, George Hsieh

INSIGHT EDITIONS

Publisher: Raoul Goff

Design: Jason Babler, Chrissy Kwasnik, Justin Allen

Editing: Jake Gerli, Jan Hughes, Mark Nichol

Production: Anna Wan, Jane Chinn, Binh Matthews

Library of Congress Cataloging-in-Publication Data available.

ISBN: 978-1-60887-063-9

REPLANTED PAPER   Insight Editions, in association with Roots
of Peace, will plant two trees for each tree used in the manufacturing of this
book. Roots of Peace is an internationally renowned humanitarian organization
dedicated to eradicating land mines worldwide and converting war-torn lands into
productive farms and wildlife habitats. Together, we will plant two million fruit
and nut trees in Afghanistan and provide farmers there with the skills and support
necessary for sustainable land use.

Manufactured in China

10 9 8 7 6 5 4 3 2 1

ART CREDITS

Brom — Pages 34, 44, 107, 109, 133, 135, 136, 139, 143

Mark Gibbons — Pages 8, 18, 20, 29 (top), 21, 23, 26, 29 (top), 31, 32, 35, 37 (middle),
39, 40, 42, 45, 47, 54, 61, 62 (right), 63 (left), 68, 83, 97, 100, 130, 132, 134, 137, 138, 142

James Gurney — Pages 17, 52, 53, 55, 56, 57, 60, 70, 71 (bottom), 88

John Howe — Page 2

Joseph Lacroix — Pages 127, 128

Alan Lee — Page 4

Victor Lee — Pages 140, 145

Christian Lichtner — Cover

Iain McCaig — Pages 27, 58, 62 (left), 76, 89, 98–99, 110

Petar Meseldžija — Pages 93, 102, 117

Jean-Baptiste Monge — Pages 10, 12, 24, 28, 33, 36, 38, 46, 49, 64–65, 73, 74, 78,
90, 91, 104, 105, 113, 114, 120, 122–123, 129

Adrian Smith — Pages 14, 22, 30, 43, 50, 63 (right), 66, 80, 115, 118, 119

now bear this burden. I console myself by remembering that you are so much stronger than I ever was—and that your great heart is young and true.

I'm sorry for so many things, Jean. Sorry that this befuddled old fool is the closest thing you've ever known for a father. Sorry that you've never had the quiet life you deserve. Sorry that you are forced to sacrifice a carefree youth and the simple joys of home and friends, all on account of my life's work—my life's obsession. In all the ways that truly matter, the needs of my life have always overshadowed your own. And now, as I sense my life drawing to a close, I am overwhelmed by regret.

Be that as it may, the one thing I want to make absolutely clear to you, dear one, is that for all the things I've seen and learned while trekking across this strange, dangerous world, there is only one truth I hold with complete certainty: that you are the single greatest joy of my life.

For all the darkness and fear we have come through together, you were always the light of hope and promise that kept me going. My child. My sweet daughter—if not by blood, then certainly through love and devotion.

I could not be any prouder of you, Jean—of the woman you've become.

Come what may, dear one, always hold fast to hope. For far beyond the crash of worlds and the unending struggle within our own frail hearts, I believe that something better lies in store for us.

A new beginning. A clean slate. A paradise . . .

. . . where we might meet again.

Love,

Uncle Deckard